S0-AFA-521

NEW DIRECTIONS
FOR
PHILANTHROPIC
FUNDRAISING

Robert E. Fogal
Ohio Presbyterian Retirement Services Foundation;
formerly of the Indiana University Center on Philanthropy
EDITOR-IN-CHIEF

FINANCIAL PRACTICES FOR EFFECTIVE FUNDRAISING

James M. Greenfield
Hoag Memorial Hospital Presbyterian
EDITOR

NUMBER 3, SPRING 1994

FINANCIAL PRACTICES FOR EFFECTIVE FUNDRAISING
James M. Greenfield (ed.)
New Directions for Philanthropic Fundraising, No. 3, Spring 1994
Robert E. Fogal, Editor-in-Chief

Microfilm copies of issues and articles are available in 16 mm and 35 mm, as well as microfiche in 105 mm, through University Microfilms Inc., 300 North Zeeb Road, Ann Arbor, Michigan 48106-1346.

ISSN 1072-172X   ISBN 0-7879-9969-5

NEW DIRECTIONS FOR PHILANTHROPIC FUNDRAISING is part of The Jossey-Bass Nonprofit Sector Series and is published quarterly by Jossey-Bass Inc., Publishers, 350 Sansome Street, San Francisco, California 94104-1310.

SUBSCRIPTIONS: Please see Ordering Information at back of book.

EDITORIAL CORRESPONDENCE should be sent to Robert E. Fogal, Ohio Presbyterian Retirement Services Foundation, OMNI Plaza, 4502 Darrow Rd., Rte. 91, Stow, OH 44224-1887.

Manufactured in the United States of America. Nearly all Jossey-Bass books, jackets, and periodicals are printed on recycled paper that contains at least 50 percent recycled waste, including 10 percent postconsumer waste. Many of our materials are also printed with vegetable-based ink; during the printing process these inks emit fewer volatile organic compounds (VOCs) than petroleum-based inks. VOCs contribute to the formation of smog.

Contents

This chapter examines performance comparisons used to demonstrate fundraising success or failure. The few data sources available for such analysis, all of which are only estimates, must be used with caution. At best, they can provide a broad overview of giving and suggest general trends and patterns.

Regulation and enforcement have limited effects on the performance of non-profit organizations. They can and do encourage responsible reporting and can be used to reinforce public confidence in legitimate fundraising activities with effective regulation of fraud and abuse.

Editor's Notes

WHILE THE PRACTICE of fundraising has not as yet achieved status as a recognized profession, it is making rapid progress in that direction. Robert Carbone (1989, p. 27) defined the ingredients necessary to achieve professionalism: "Autonomy of decision making; A systematic body of knowledge and skills; Self-regulation and collegial standard setting; Commitment to and identification with the profession; Altruism and dedication to service; and A code of ethics with accompanying sanctions."

This series, New Directions in Philanthropic Fundraising, initiated by the Indiana University Center on Philanthropy, speaks to the level of professionalism already attained while identifying the remaining areas in need of development for professional standing. Within "a systematic body of knowledge and skills" are common management practices built upon established principles such as found in economics, accounting, statistics, and the law. Widespread acceptance of the unique methods and techniques of fundraising practice will require more work than this series alone can provide, but its presence speaks eloquently of progress already made and the commitment of many practitioners to push forward toward the goal of professionalism. The seven authors in this volume, all distinguished in their respective fields, together add considerable momentum to that movement.

Robert Payton (1988) defined philanthropy as voluntary action for the public good. Fundraising, to be successful, requires management of communications that encourage the public to share, with confidence, some of their discretionary resources for the urgent and relevant needs of others. "For organizations willing to make the kinds of commitment required to conduct sophisticated, coordinated programs, success is virtually assured. Those who are not willing to apply themselves systematically and professionally will continue to be frustrated, puzzled about why their organization cannot raise money when others all around them are reporting new high levels of support. Time does not stand still for organizations that offer excuses and rationalizations rather than effort. The success of too many organizations in America proves otherwise" (Broce, 1986, p. 16).

The chapters in this volume, "Financial Practices for Effective Fundraising," begin with Richard Steinberg's clear call for nonprofit organizations to use professional economic measures, such as optimization and economies of scale, in their fundraising campaigns and to define budgets for fundraising as investments. He also cautions against use of cost-benefit ratio analysis. Nonprofit organizations are dependent on philanthropic practices, but their fundraising staffs act more on intuition and have yet to investigate and incorporate traditional economic analysis within their management practice.

This call for increased study of economic measures also suggests increased knowledge of accounting practice. The 1990s are active times for accounting change, and considerable attention is being given to nonprofit organizations. The Financial Accounting Standards Board (FASB) has issued several standards and guidelines relating to financial statements and contributions, as well as new reporting procedures for such common activities as pledges (unconditional promises to give with the payments due in future years) and contributed services, to name just two. In Chapter Two, Richard F. Larkin discusses applications of these new standards to fundraising practice; his comments are valuable for their timing as well as explanatory content. He also speaks to the continuing confusion sparked by FASB over fundraising expense. Until nonprofit organizations receive better instruction from the accounting profession in this area, the relationships among budgets, accounting for and reporting of gifts, analysis of performance, and consistent public reporting will remain undefined.

Fundraising is a distinct type of business and is more often resource development than money raising because it is so highly dependent on voluntary human resources for effectiveness as well as efficiency. Arthur S. Collier, in Chapter Three, demonstrates how these latter two features of fundraising can be measured. He also illustrates how to display these data to demonstrate the levels of profitability and productivity achieved. Collier provides a variety of measurement tools and reporting formats to assist our understanding of performance characteristics for each of the several methods that comprise routine fundraising activities for a nonprofit organization.

Fundraising is much more than just asking for money. It is an investment, and, like all investments, its total returns are achieved in the future. Wesley E. Lindahl, in Chapter Four, offers several different econometric techniques that can be applied to forecast future fundraising performance. Investments in fundraising are appreciated assets with continuous "pay out" each year and with multiple yields in current and future years. Board members and management staff often focus only on current cash results, perhaps because their attention first must be given to the task of meeting current fiscal objectives. The resources provided to fundraising must be viewed in terms of time-delayed results to appreciate greater consequences than budget expended against cash received. Models designed to forecast future returns on fundraising budgets are illustrated to demonstrate the wisdom of these investments and to guide the strategic planning process.

Beyond an understanding of the effectiveness, efficiency, profitability, and productivity of fundraising practice, the next challenge in fundraising economics is to convince the public that their continued investments in giving, through multiple gifts year after year, are wise. In Chapter Five, Gary A. Tobin reports on a multiyear study of major-donor motives for giving, to whom they give, and their attitudes about fundraising and administrative costs. Major donors are the most important people to convince to invest in philanthropy, for without their capacity for support nonprofit organizations cannot progress beyond "pocket change" for current purposes. Major donors, of course, must be fully convinced that their dollars will achieve maximum effect. Each organization must be able to demonstrate how it is efficient and effective in the use of their money.

Reporting of gift results has always been an important part of the fundraising enterprise. Fundraising professionals are constantly asked, "How much money did you raise?" Today, there are more questions, such as "How much did it cost to raise it?" and "Are your costs reasonable?" and "How do your costs compare to other nonprofit organizations?" New accounting rules, along with new federal and state laws and regulations, require greater public disclosure of fundraising results. However, statistical analysis of fundraising performance data has received only limited attention. In their defense, fundraising professionals have been handicapped by the absence of standard measurement tools. But they have also been slow to investigate new sources of national data, such as the *Nonprofit Almanac,* a publication of INDEPENDENT SECTOR. Most fund raisers rely on *Giving USA,* the annual report prepared by the American Association of Fund Raising Counsel Trust for Philanthropy. In Chapter Six, Nathan Weber provides an insightful discussion of how to use (and how not to abuse) national statistics as an evaluation tool.

State governments have been active in regulating fundraising practice, chiefly dealing with fraud and public protection. In his review of the role of state legislation and regulation pertaining to fundraising, in Chapter Seven, David E. Ormstedt, a twenty-year veteran in state regulation of nonprofit organizations, suggests that regulation has been less than optimally effective where constitutional protection is a priority concern. There are areas where the states can and should be active in support of fundraising practices, including disclosure. There is also room for increased responsible reporting by the private sector. The debate here is not about disclosure as a requirement but rather about the data to be made public, the need for public understanding of these data, and the lack of uniformity in data requirements by the states. The state also must protect the public from fraud and abuse, including illicit fundraising practices. Nonprofit organizations must work actively with state authorities to resolve these valid issues, because this cooperation will improve public confidence and trust in fundraising activities and also help to educate the public on how to recognize fraudulent and abusive practices.

Regulations have a unique way of getting everyone's attention. Successful fundraising depends on public confidence and trust and the ability of fund raisers to demonstrate by their results the effective use of gift dollars for public benefit. Nonprofit organizations must adopt established economic practices and apply standard accounting procedures in all of their fiscal reports prepared for public scrutiny with the aim to improve public understanding. With better data available and a better public understanding of what performance criteria demonstrate, donors will be able to make their independent gift decisions with confidence that the philanthropic organizations selected will be efficient and effective in achieving their charitable purposes to the benefit of those in need.

James M. Greenfield
Editor

References

Broce, T. E. *Fund Raising: The Guide to Raising Money from Private Sources.* (2nd ed.) Norman: University of Oklahoma Press, 1986.

Carbone, R. *Fund Raising as a Profession.* College Park, Md.: Clearinghouse for Research on Fund Raising, 1989.

Payton, R. L. *Philanthropy: Voluntary Action for the Public Good.* New York: American Council on Education, 1988.

JAMES M. GREENFIELD, *a fundraising executive for thirty-two years, is senior vice president of development and community relations at Hoag Memorial Hospital Presbyterian, Newport Beach, California. A frequent lecturer on fundraising management, finance, and cost-effectiveness, he is the author of* Fund-Raising: Evaluating and Managing the Fund Development Process *(New York: Wiley, 1991).*

This chapter illustrates the many uses of economics in the design of fundraising campaigns and in donor decision making, providing a nontechnical introduction to the subject for nonprofit managers and fundraising professionals.

1

Economics and philanthropy: A marriage of necessity for nonprofit organizations

Richard Steinberg

FUNDRAISING is not simply a matter of gathering funds. Nor is economics simply the science of accumulating money. Both concern broader issues of scarcity and trade-offs. Surely, fund raisers care about monetary issues when they decide on (or request from management) a solicitation budget and consider how to divide this budget among alternative fundraising techniques. However, trade-offs enter the picture when one strategy leads to immediate donations while another leads to streams of future donations, or when one sacrifices the right to conduct an independent campaign in order to secure the benefits from a united fundraising organization such as United Way. Fund raisers must also be concerned with nonmonetary matters such as volunteer recruitment and potential conflicts between the methods chosen to raise funds and the attainment of the organization's charitable mission. Donors must consider strictly financial matters such as the effect of their giving on their personal tax liabilities, but they must also consider

NEW DIRECTIONS FOR PHILANTHROPIC FUNDRAISING, NO. 3, SPRING 1994 © JOSSEY-BASS PUBLISHERS

trade-offs when deciding how to split their scarce available funds among donations to competing causes, competing organizations serving similar causes, and personal consumption.

Economics is the study of how scarce resources are allocated among competing uses to satisfy human wants. It matters not whether resources or services are bought and sold; as long as there is scarcity and the consequent necessity for trading off competing wants, the tools of economics can be helpful. Thus, in environmental economics, one learns how to value environmental amenities that are not (directly) traded in markets, such as clean air, clean water, and the preservation of endangered species. One then learns to trade off these amenities against jobs and the production of marketed goods and services to foster economic growth in its broadest sense. In public economics, one learns how to conduct a broader cost-benefit analysis so that decisions about public projects and regulations are based on social values in addition to those values reflected in the prices at which goods are traded.

Many fund raisers, development officers, and nonprofit managers have an intuitive understanding of economics but little formal training in the subject. Perhaps this reflects a belief that economics is solely about market values and therefore useful only to profit-seeking firms and entrepreneurs. Truth be known, most introductory courses in economics cover only these subjects, leaving students with a distorted appreciation of the subject. However, economics is about more than money, and I believe that nonprofit managers need economics as much as do for-profit managers. Certainly, intuitive insight and experience will always be central requirements for good management; mechanistic application of economic principles is not always possible and rarely appropriate (in either the for-profit or philanthropic worlds). Nonetheless, by making managers' intuitive understanding of scarcity more explicit, economics training permits them to deal with trade-offs in a more consistent fashion, gather and statistically analyze data that are truly useful, assess the productivity of alternative strategies, and generally improve management practice.

In this chapter, I discuss three primary tools of economists— optimization, valuation, and econometrics—and show how they can be fruitfully applied to common problems in campaign design. I then show how economics can be useful from the donor perspective. My goal in both cases is to clarify the importance of economics. I leave the technical details of implementation to other chapters in this volume, other publications, and even future researchers.

Applications of economics to fundraising

The economic approach provides decision rules that enable a fund raiser to optimize a campaign, techniques to combine seemingly incommensurate types of costs and benefits into one overall index, and statistical methods to obtain needed data.

Optimization

One of the primary tools provided by economics is the ability to calculate and characterize the constrained optimum. Thus, for-profit firms learn how to choose a price and production level to maximize profits, given consumer willingness to buy at various possible prices and the costs of producing various quantities. They also learn how to choose a mixture of inputs (workers, machines, raw materials) that will minimize the costs of producing the chosen quantity. Consumers learn how to choose a set of purchases to maximize their well-being given limited income, or how to allocate their limited time across sleep, paid labor, and leisure time. The tool of constrained optimization is no less relevant to fundraising.

Optimization of fundraising. There are at least seven categories of optimization problems faced when designing a fundraising campaign: choosing the overall solicitation budget, dividing this sum across alternative techniques and media, dividing this sum between new-donor acquisition and donor retention, choosing the level of effort and resources to target to individual donors and classes of donors, choosing the types of workers to run the campaign (volunteer or paid), choosing whether to conduct the campaign with internal resources or to hire out with an external fundraising counsel (and, if external, choosing contract terms), and choosing how to finance a campaign (borrowing versus retained earnings). To some extent, these decisions interact— obviously, the best level for the total solicitation budget depends on the ways in which one anticipates allocating this sum—but much intuition and guidance can be provided by considering the problems separately.

First, one needs to choose a solicitation budget, presumably, to maximize the net returns from fundraising (that is, donations minus solicitation expenditures or the amount left over for service provision). Donations are only partly under the control of an individual organization, depending chiefly on the level of competition from other charities, the state of donor finances and the economy more generally, the intensity of need for the organization's services and the ability of others (such as government agencies) to meet these needs, and the social climate (sense of community, trendiness of the cause, and so forth). Nonetheless, the level of solicitation spending is under the control of the organization, and there is a best level to spend for each set of external realities. At this best level, dollars devoted to fundraising do not come at the expense of service provision, for the resource pie is sufficiently enlarged to more than make up for the solicitation slice.

One needs to know how to divide this budget across alternative techniques (including direct mail, telemarketing, media, door-to-door, and other methods) to minimize the expenditure necessary to raise a given amount of money (or, equivalently, to maximize the donations received from a given expenditure on solicitation). One also needs to know how to target resources to individual donors and classes of donors: Should selected prime prospects be targeted for intensive effort, and how intensive should that effort be? How should efforts be split between prospecting for new donors and securing the continuing contributions of previous donors? Should certain communities receive more attention than others within the organization's region?

Once the budget is decided and split among alternative uses, the organization must make production decisions. Volunteers have a low dollar cost, so they are often employed in fundraising campaigns in an effort to secure real efficiency and to make the fundraising cost ratio appear better. However, volunteer time is scarce, so the full opportunity cost of employing volunteers in fundraising is considerably higher than the dollar cost. Volunteer time devoted to fundraising is unavailable for service provision; it might be better, in some circumstances, to replace paid service professionals with volunteers and replace volunteer fund raisers with paid professionals (Steinberg, 1992).

The decision about whether to conduct an in-house campaign or contract out (and, if so, under what terms) also involves trade-offs that can be analyzed with the tool of optimization. Although external fundraising counsel require a markup on costs to make their efforts personally rewarding, there are corresponding efficiencies that may reduce their total opportunity cost below that of in-house campaigns. Nonprofit boards of directors and chief executive officers rarely have sufficient expertise to keep their campaigns at the forefront of fundraising proficiency, and the development of such expertise would distract them from their charitable missions, which involve the provision of services and not the raising of funds. Nonprofit organizations, especially smaller ones, may lack experience and be unable to secure economies of scale.

If the decision is made to go outside, there are trade-offs to consider in contract provisions. For example, fundraising counsel may request the exclusive right to market mailing lists developed as a result of the contract. In return, they offer the nonprofit organization lower fees, an interest-free loan to finance the campaign, and campaign insurance to guarantee that the campaign will not lose money. Both the fundraising counsel and nonprofit organization must trade off such costs and benefits before a mutually beneficial optimal contract can be designed.

Finally, the decision must be made about how to finance the campaign. Far too many organizations use available funds, rather than prospective net benefits, to decide the scale of their fundraising efforts. Management must be better educated: Sometimes available funds are better invested in the stock market and real estate than in fundraising; sometimes the benefits to solicitation are such that the organization is well advised to secure a costly loan to make funds available (either independently or implicitly through a contract with external fundraising counsel). In either case, the organization must trade current costs against anticipated future benefits in order to optimize its time stream of service provision.

One category of optimization problems is much more complex. Sometimes there are strategic interactions between different fund seekers or between fund seekers and donors. If a charity covertly cripples its private-donor solicitation efforts and pleads poverty as a basis for the granting of federal funds, the impact of this strategy depends on the strategy taken by government funders, who may respond with a matching requirement. If a new fundraising gimmick is developed, the first charity to use it may profit enormously, whereas donors are jaded when others imitate it. These types of strategic interactions, where the optimal strategy for one depends on the strategy chosen by others, require the more sophisticated tools of game theory. Game theory has been applied to a variety of business and social problems (price wars versus collusion, innovation races, poker, nuclear war deterrence), but the literature on fundraising has not yet made much use of this powerful tool (see Dixit and Nalebuff, 1991, for an informative introduction to the power of game theory in a variety of settings).

Goals. To apply the methods of optimization, one must be clear, precise, and complete about the organization's objectives. Most charities probably want to maximize the net returns from fundraising, for this is a prerequisite to maximizing the level of charitable services that they can provide. Elsewhere (Steinberg, 1986a), I have called this objective "service maximization." However, service maximization is not the only goal a charity might have. A charity may wish to avoid certain high-return fundraising techniques because these techniques are regarded as deceptive or unethical, or because they employ "high pressure." In this case, the organization really has two goals—to raise maximal funds and to use only "acceptable" techniques for raising them—and these goals likely come into conflict. The charity's objective is not fully and precisely spelled out until the analyst can specify the goal trade-offs that the charity is prepared to make.

As one extreme, the charity might eschew "tainted money" obtained through unacceptable techniques, regardless of the size of the net returns or the minor nature of the "infraction." Most charities would like to believe that this extreme correctly describes their objectives, but it is unclear how many organizations always adhere to this principle. The other extreme, maximizing net funds raised regardless of the means used to obtain them, is never asserted as the organizational objective and probably characterizes few (if any) nonprofit organizations. Most organizations probably fall somewhere in the middle of these two extremes. Most would probably benefit from an explicit, if internal, discussion of organizational values and trade-offs. Regardless, the optimization analysis cannot be rigorously completed until the exact and complete objective is specified.

Other goals have been asserted in the literature. For example, Tullock (1966) asserted that some nonprofit organizations might wish to maximize the gross returns from fundraising, spending an additional dollar on solicitation even if it results in only an additional penny in donations (thus subtracting ninety-nine cents from service provision). Maximal gross returns would maximize the budget under the control of the chief executive officer and board of directors, perhaps bringing them power, prestige, and higher salaries if not the satisfaction of having best advanced the charitable mission of the organization. This alternative objective of "budget maximization" is sensible but appears to be quite rare.

Taking the fundraising techniques as given (so that trade-offs with acceptability are not analyzed), I statistically analyzed the fundraising performances of several hundred nonprofit organizations to determine which of these competing objectives better explained the data. That is, I uncovered the objective functions that ostensibly explained the organizations' actions, the closest one can get to uncovering the organizations' real objectives. I found that the average social welfare, arts and culture, or education organization acted like a service maximizer, whereas the average hospital acted like a budget maximizer (Steinberg, 1986a). It is comforting to know that budget maximization appears comparatively rare, but each organization must decide on its own objective and not rely on statistical averages.

Ratios are irrelevant. The basic lesson from optimization analysis is that ratios do not matter, and this lesson applies equally well to fund raisers (see, for example, Steinberg, 1991, and the references therein). Consider this example of two alternative solicitation budgets. The first budget of $10,000 will produce $50,000 in donations and provide a 500 percent ratio return ($40,000 actual net return). The second budget of $100,000 will produce $200,000, a 200 percent ratio return ($100,000 actual net return). If a charity wished to maximize the *rate* of return on its fundraising investment, it would choose the first budget; if it cared about maximizing its resources for providing charitable services, it would choose the second. Another common and equivalent way of looking at things, minimization of the fundraising cost ratio (solicitation expenditures divided by contributions received), is no more helpful; the ratio for the first budget (20 percent) looks better than the ratio for the superior second budget (50 percent). Except by an incredible coincidence, the level of solicitation expenditures that best supports service provision is different from the level that maximizes the ratio of return or the level that minimizes the fundraising cost ratio, so the latter statistics are not helpful in planning campaigns.

This basic insight ignores some complications. Rose-Ackerman (1982) and I (Steinberg, 1986b) examined the complications that arise when donors base their decisions, in part, on the fundraising cost ratio (but see the discussion below). I (Steinberg, 1990) have also discussed some of the complications that arise when executive compensation is directly dependent on fundraising performance or when contracts with external fundraising counsel obligate that a fixed percentage of receipts go to the fund raiser. The basic conclusion from these analyses is that fundraising cost ratios are helpful for making management decisions, but the relationship between these ratios and management decision rules is complex. In general, one would not want to minimize the fundraising cost ratio even when these complications apply.

Of course, for a fixed solicitation budget, the lower the fundraising cost ratio, the higher the level of net returns. Thus, for example, one would prefer an expenditure of $100,000 that produced $200,000 over the same total expenditure, used in a different way, to produce only $175,000 by either criterion. For a fixed budget, the two decision criteria are identical. However, ratios of return for investments on specific fundraising techniques do not provide guidance on how to split up a given fixed solicitation budget among alternative uses.

To see the irrelevance of ratios in allocating a solicitation budget, consider this example. Suppose an organization splits its $100,000 budget evenly across two communities. In the first community, it raises $125,000; in the second, $75,000. Although the organization got a 250 percent return on its investment in the first community and only a 150 percent return in the second, we cannot tell whether the budget should be split differently. It might be that the first campaign has virtually reached the saturation level, so even if all $100,000 were spent there (eliminating the $75,000 stemming from the second community), only $130,000 would be raised in the first community and in total. Clearly, productivity ratios provide no guidance in allocating a solicitation budget across alternative uses.

Incremental or "marginal" returns matter. When one is maximizing, one is looking for the top of the hill. To find the top of the hill, simply look around and find out which way is uphill, then go there. If we find ourselves on level ground, and there is no direction in which we can go that carries us higher, we must be at the top. The procedure for minimizing is similar: To find the bottom of the valley, move downhill until all is level. This hill-climbing analogy provides the essential insight into optimization, with incremental returns playing the role of slope. Positive incremental returns allow us to climb uphill; zero incremental returns place us on a level surface; negative incremental returns bring us downhill.

Economists use the word *marginal* as a synonym for *incremental.* When economists say that the marginal return to solicitation is $4, they are not using the word's other definition to dismiss the importance of solicitation; rather, they are asserting that an additional dollar spent on solicitation would increase donations by $4, so spending more brings one up the donations slope.

Ratios are uninformative, but marginal returns can guide one to the optimum. Budget-maximizing nonprofit organizations need only follow this simple rule to accomplish their goals: Choose a level of fundraising expenditures such that the marginal return equals zero. At any other level of expenditures, they can climb the donations slope through incremental adjustments: If the marginal return is positive, an increase in expenditures will increase donations; if negative, a decrease in expenditures points them uphill.

The rule for service maximizers is only slightly more complex. Service maximizers wish to climb the hill of *net* donations (donations minus solicitation expenditures), and so they must choose a level of expenditure such that the marginal *gross* return equals one. When the marginal return equals one, the increase in beneficial donations from an uphill climb exactly cancels out the increase in detrimental solicitation costs, so the service maximizer is on the level plateau at the top of the net return mountain. Starting anywhere else, the fund raiser could climb higher: If the marginal return exceeds one, an increase in expenditures more than pays for itself and adds to resources available for service provision; if the marginal return is less than one, a decrease in expenditures cuts costs more than it cuts donations, again freeing resources for service provision. (Fund raisers who choose budgets such that the marginal returns are less than one can indeed be said to be "over the hill.")

Some object to this rule, wondering why they should bother spending a dollar to raise a dollar. The answer is simple: Only the last dollar spent was a wash—every previous dollar more than paid for itself and supported services. If the charity demanded a higher return on each dollar spent (including the last few), it would be shortchanging those who rely on it for service provision.

The rule for allocating a solicitation budget among competing uses is only slightly more complicated: Split the budget so that it is entirely spent and so that the marginal returns from each selected technique are equal to one another. The reason for this complication is again the nature of the hill. Each dollar spent on one fundraising technique within a fixed budget is a dollar less spent on some other technique. If the extra dollars raised from marginal expenditures on the first technique exactly counteract the loss in donations following the cutback in spending on competing techniques, one is on the level plateau at the top. Conversely, if the marginal return to, say, direct media is $3.00 while the marginal return to telemarketing is $1.25, a reallocation of a dollar's solicitation expenditure from telemarketing to direct media would increase net contributions by $1.75, and one should keep climbing in that direction until the returns equal each other.

A little bit of knowledge is dangerous. There are additional complications, spelled out elsewhere (Steinberg, 1991; the chapters by Larkin, Collier, Lindahl, and Tobin in this volume, for example), of which managers need to be aware before applying these rules. However, the basic insight remains robust: managerial intuition is best guided by estimates of the marginal returns to overall investment and investment in specific categories of solicitation.

Valuation

The benefits of fundraising are not restricted to monetary returns. Campaigns might attract additional volunteers, indirectly further the organization's service goals, attract in-kind gifts or gifts with substantial restrictions, or result in future monetary gifts. All of these outcomes must be weighed on a common scale so that they can be included in the marginal returns that guide the organization to optimality.

Economists use dollars as the common scale of measurement, but with a twist. Rather than use the actual dollar costs to measure gross benefits, economists use the organization's *maximum willingness to pay*. The more one is willing to pay to secure the services of, say, a volunteer, the more valuable that volunteer must be to the organization. In turn, willingness to pay is constrained by the cost of available alternatives. For example, if the value of one hour of volunteer time to the organization exactly equals the value of forty minutes' labor by a paid professional whose wage is $15 per hour, the organization's maximum willingness to pay for the volunteer is $10.

The organization's net benefit is the difference between the gross benefit (maximum willingness to pay) and the "payment" required to obtain that resource. Thus, continuing the example above, if a volunteer hour can be recruited and retained for $2 an hour, the net marginal value of this volunteer hour is $8. In determining the necessary payment, a broad view of the term should be taken. We have already seen, in this example, that it can cost something to employ a worker even at zero wages, but the issue can be even broader. If available volunteer hours are limited (that is, if the organization cannot recruit as many volunteers as it wants at some fixed cost per volunteer), then the organization is also "paying" for volunteer hours devoted to, say, fundraising in an opportunity-cost sense: Those volunteers can no longer provide value to the firm in service delivery. Continuing the example, if the volunteer used in service delivery provided services that would otherwise cost the firm $10 per hour to provide, the true net value of the volunteer used in fundraising would be negative $2, and this "free" volunteer is better used elsewhere.

Sometimes, a campaign fosters the desired service as an inherent side effect, independently of money raised. This is especially true for advocacy organizations or those whose mission encompasses public education. If an organization's fundraising literature informs or persuades the public on the organizational mission, then the organization's willingness to pay for the accomplishment of this mission counts as a marginal benefit to solicitation and should be added to the marginal donation returns for optimization purposes. Generally, the organization would not be willing to pay more to piggyback an educational message on a solicitation request than it would to send the message through a separate mailing, so we know that the value is less than or equal to this alternative cost. However, one cannot be more precise without a detailed understanding of organizational objectives.

Sometimes a gift is restricted and can only be used for specified purposes. If the size of the gift is less than or equal to the amount that the charity was otherwise intending to spend on that purpose, then the restriction has no impact and the size of the gift correctly indicates the gift's value. However, large restricted gifts might force the charity to spend its resources on less-favored outputs, so the true value of the gift to the charity is less than the gift's dollar amount. Once again, the organization's willingness to pay for the mandated service (which is less than what the gift mandates to be spent) represents the true value.

Solicitation efforts this year, especially those for recruiting new donors, will have effects on donations for many years in the future, and these benefits must be evaluated and added to the immediate monetary returns prior to optimization (see Lindahl, this volume, for further discussion). The basic tool taught to for-profit managers and financiers can be applied here without modification: Future costs and benefits should be converted to their present discounted value. The basic idea here is that the borrowing or lending of money provides a relevant alternative that bounds the present value of future money. For example, if I obtain 10 percent annual interest by putting my money in the bank, then the maximum amount that I would be willing to pay today for a dollar to be delivered one year from now is roughly ninety-one cents. I would not pay a full dollar now, because I would lose use of that dollar for a year and hence lose the dollar and ten cents I could otherwise obtain by putting that money in the bank. If I get the future dollar for ninety-one cents today, I do equally well keeping my money or purchasing the right to the future money; if I get the future dollar for less than ninety-one cents, I come out ahead in the transaction. Thought of another way, if I borrowed ninety-one cents today to secure the future dollar, I would just break even in a year after repaying the loan. Thus, whether thought of as taking a loan or providing a loan to the bank, ninety-one cents is my maximum willingness to pay for the future dollar.

This same logic applies, with increasing computational complexity, to donations received in stages over, say, the next ten years due to today's solicitation efforts, and so present discounted value can be applied to complex trusts and bequests. Uncertainty also enters into the calculation, for the organization may not be sure exactly when the money will be received, how much it will be, or whether the donor will back out of his or her pledge (particularly for bequests). Finally, if the organization is unable to borrow or lend and is short of retained funds, the interest rate no longer provides a relevant alternative that bounds its willingness to pay. If future donations are uncertain or capital is currently scarce, future money becomes even less valuable and should be discounted by a factor that is higher than the interest rate and reflects the organization's views toward risk.

Econometrics

It is one thing to instruct a development officer to choose a budget that leads to a marginal donative product of one, quite another to figure out how to implement this advice. One way is through statistical analysis of past campaign performances of the organization and other similarly situated organizations. Econometrics is the combination of economics and statistics. Like its sister hybrids from other social sciences (such as sociometrics and psychometrics), econometrics can provide the necessary information for implementing optimization rules.

Econometric analysis would be unnecessary if we lived in a much simpler world, where donations depended only on solicitation expenditures and did so in a perfectly stable way. Then we could locate the optimal solicitation level through repeated application of the "differencing test" (Steinberg, 1991). Here is how the differencing test works. An organization calculates the change in donations received between two years ago and one year ago and divides this difference by the change in solicitation expenditures. The result exactly equals (under our unrealistic simplifying assumption) the average marginal product of fundraising over this range; so if this number is greater than one, the organization spent too little and should choose a larger expenditure this year. Next year, the analogous calculation proceeds, and if the result is still greater than one, the budget should be increased further; if the result is less than one, the organization has overshot the optimum and should choose a level of spending in between the two previous levels; if the result is approximately equal to one, the organization should continue spending the same amount indefinitely.

The problem with the differencing test in the real world is that donations change for a variety of reasons other than the change in fundraising expenditures (change in donor income, in the need for services, and so forth), so the marginal product estimate is confounded with a variety of other effects. If fundraising were a physical science, one could run a controlled experiment to isolate the independent influence of fundraising on donations; but it is unclear whether such an experiment is feasible for fundraising and whether the laboratory experience would translate into the real world. Although economists are, for the first time, conducting controlled laboratory experiments to better understand other market behaviors (typically using undergraduate economics majors as subjects), statistical analysis of data generated in the uncontrolled real world has a longer pedigree and more general acceptance.

With econometrics, one estimates the likely effects of the other factors and subtracts them to estimate the independent influence of the factor of interest. Thus, we can artificially and probabilistically hold constant the income level, spending by government, tax incentives for giving, and other confounding effects to isolate which part of the change in donations between two years is due to the change in fundraising expenditures and so estimate the marginal product.

Econometric results are always "best guesses," but they are better than stabs in the dark. The differencing method remains a useful first step, but econometrics provides better estimates when sufficient data are available. Results are more persuasive if there are many observations and if there are measurements of the most important confounding variables. Under some circumstances, observations made by other organizations can be combined with one's own experience to improve the quality of the estimates. Elsewhere (Steinberg, 1991), I have provided a more detailed introduction to econometric applications to fundraising and have summarized available empirical studies employing these methods.

Econometrics can be used for forecasting as well as aiding optimization. Donor income and the tax treatment of donations are confounding variables when one is trying to estimate the marginal product of fundraising; but if one can determine the independent influences of these variables, one can obtain better forecasts of the likely level of donations in future years. Econometric techniques do not just remove confounding influences, they simultaneously estimate the numerical impact of each, providing the information necessary for forecasting and for answering "what if" questions (see Clotfelter, 1985, for a comprehensive introduction to the use of econometric methods to forecast and simulate giving).

Applications of economics to donor decisions

Donors might wish to optimize, obtaining maximal beneficial results from their donations. The tools of economics can be helpful here too. I consider four applications below: evaluating the impact of tax subsidies, using fundraising cost ratios to choose which charity to support, using information on management incentives to choose which charity to support, and assessing the value of tied gifts such as donations to United Way.

Donations to some charities are tax deductible for some donors; donations to others are not. How should donors regard this difference in the tax treatment? Economists suggest that the difference amounts to a price decrease for the latter category. Here is why. If one donates a dollar to an eligible organization and can itemize on the tax return, then taxable income is reduced by that dollar, so tax liabilities are reduced by one's marginal tax rate. For example, those in the 30 percent bracket would reduce their tax liability by thirty cents per dollar donated, in effect allowing them to contribute a dollar at a personal cost of only seventy cents. Donations to noneligible nonprofits have a personal cost of one dollar per dollar given. Donors should respond to this difference in the same way they respond to other price differences, "buying" the more expensive charitable product only if there is some compensating difference in merit.

Do fundraising cost ratios enter the effective price of giving as well? One might think so, and the first economists to analyze the problem assumed that this is the way things work (Rose-Ackerman, 1982). If 30 percent of donations go to solicitation expenses, it seems like there would be a personal cost of $1.30 in order to increment charitable service expenditures by $1.00. However, this argument does not withstand careful analysis, as demonstrated in Steinberg (1986b, 1988–1989, 1991). The logical error is that there is no reason why an organization that spent 30 percent of earlier contributions should continue to spend 30 percent of new receipts. For example, both service- and budget-maximizing organizations pick their solicitation budgets in fixed dollar terms (rather than a fixed percentage of receipts) and would not divert any portion of marginal donations to fundraising expenditures. Thus, for both types of organizations (neglecting tax considerations), the price of giving is $1.00 regardless of the fundraising cost share. For other types of nonprofit organizations, the price of giving can differ from $1.00, but there is no easy relation between fundraising cost ratios and the price that donors would be able to calculate and use.

Informed donors make better decisions if the information given is actually useful. The point of my argument above is that fundraising cost ratios are not useful to rational donors, so mandated point-of-solicitation disclosure of fundraising cost ratios at best accomplish nothing and at worst confuse donors and lead them to make worse decisions.

The situation is different if an incentive-compensation scheme is used, either internally or by contract with external fundraising counsel, that promises a fixed share of funds raised as a reward to the fund raiser. Then, the price of giving is indeed higher when the promised percentage is increased, and donors would do well to adjust their donations accordingly (Steinberg, 1990). Thus, economic analysis can help refine the use of point-of-solicitation disclosure laws (recommended, for example, in Ormstedt, this volume).

When one gives to a united fundraising organization (UFO) such as United Way, one is, in effect, supporting a variety of charities in proportions determined by this pass-through organization. Such donations appear irrational at first, for there is very little chance that the UFO will divide an individual's contributions among charities in the way that he or she prefers and some chance that a portion of the donations will go to charities that the individual actively dislikes. Yet, there are corresponding efficiencies that can make such contributions worthwhile (Fisher, 1977; Rose-Ackerman, 1980). First, the UFO saves individual donors the trouble of doing their own "homework" in investigating the merits and efficiency of alternative nonprofit recipients and requiring that recipients meet standards of accountability. Second, although individual donors may be forced to contribute to charities that they do not like, they are compensated when other donors are similarly forced to contribute to causes that the first donors support. Finally, UFOs typically make giving convenient by offering a payroll deduction option.

Conclusion

Nonprofit managers and fundraising professionals make economics decisions every day when deciding on solicitation budgets, how to spend those budgets, and how to use labor and volunteer resources. Donors make economics decisions when choosing recipients of their gifts. Training in economics, appropriately generalized to incorporate the special realities of the nonprofit sector, can help these decision makers make better choices and advance the charitable missions of donors and organizations.

References

Clotfelter, C. *Federal Tax Policy and Charitable Giving*. Chicago: University of Chicago Press, 1985.

Dixit, A. K., and Nalebuff, B. J. *Thinking Strategically: The Competitive Edge in Business, Politics, and Everyday Life*. New York: Norton, 1991.

Fisher, F. "On Donor Sovereignty and United Charities." *American Economic Review*, 1977, *67*, 632–638.

Rose-Ackerman, S. "United Charities: An Economic Analysis." *Public Policy*, 1980, *28*, 323–350.

Rose-Ackerman, S. "Charitable Giving and Excessive Fundraising." *Quarterly Journal of Economics*, 1982, *97*, 193–212.

Steinberg, R. "The Revealed Objective Functions of Nonprofit Firms." *Rand Journal of Economics*, 1986a, *17* (4), 508–526.

Steinberg, R. "Should Donors Care About Fundraising?" In S. Rose-Ackerman (ed.), *The Economics of Nonprofit Institutions: Studies in Structure and Policy*. New York: Oxford University Press, 1986b.

Steinberg, R. "Economic Perspectives on Regulation of Charitable Solicitation." *Case Western Reserve Law Review*, 1988–1989, *39* (3), 775–797.

Steinberg, R. "Profits and Incentive Compensation in Nonprofit Firms." *Nonprofit Management and Leadership*, 1990, *1* (2), 137–152.

Steinberg, R. "The Economics of Fund Raising." In D. F. Burlingame and L. J. Hulse (eds.), *Taking Fund Raising Seriously: Advancing the Profession and Practice of Raising Money*. San Francisco: Jossey-Bass, 1991.

Steinberg, R. *Regulation of Charity Fundraising: Unintended Consequences*. Department of Economics Working Papers, no. 92-11. Indianapolis: Economics Department, Indiana University/Purdue University, 1992.

Tullock, G. "Information Without Profit." *Papers on Non-Market Decision Making*, 1966, *1*, 141–159.

RICHARD STEINBERG *is associate professor of economics and adjunct professor of philanthropic studies at Indiana University-Purdue University, Indianapolis.*

This chapter provides fund raisers with important information needed to be fully effective: accounting principles related to gifts and fundraising expenses, the use of financial data, and some of the federal tax rules affecting charitable giving.

2

Accounting issues relating to fundraising

Richard F. Larkin

ACCOUNTING IS IMPORTANT to fundraising for a variety of reasons. First, the results of fundraising—gifts—are reported in donees' (and sometimes in donors') financial reports. Second, those reports are used by many donors to help decide on whether and how much to give, as well as by regulators and evaluation agencies to assess the performance of donees. Third, federal tax rules restrict (to some extent) what donors and donees can do.

Donors as well as donees should always be aware of the accounting, reporting, and tax rules affecting their activities. Donees will raise more money if they consider donors' concerns. Donors will have their gifts used more effectively if they structure the gifts with donees' constraints in mind. Both groups will more greatly benefit society if tax rules are observed.

NEW DIRECTIONS FOR PHILANTHROPIC FUNDRAISING, NO. 3, SPRING 1994 © JOSSEY-BASS PUBLISHERS

Accounting for gifts

The accounting issues related to gifts are whether to record certain types, when to record the asset and the revenue, how to record gifts, how to show them in the financial statements. These issues are discussed here under the topics of pledges, revenue, restricted gifts, split-interest gifts, noncash gifts, donor tax deductions, pass-through gifts, and donor accounting. Relevant tax rules are noted.

In fall 1993, the Financial Accounting Standards Board (FASB) issued new accounting standards for gifts and certain other matters related to not-for-profit entities (Financial Accounting Standards Board, 1993a, 1993b). These new standards will take effect in 1995.

Pledges

A pledge is a promise to give in the future. The pledge may be unconditional (that is, dependent only on the passage of time to become due) or conditional (that is, dependent on some future event or events, other than the passage of time, to become binding on the donor). Examples of conditions are raising of a specified "matching" amount, occurrence of a natural disaster such as an earthquake, and approval by a regulatory agency for a donee to proceed with some program activity.

By current accounting rules, conditional pledges are not recorded by the donor or donee until the condition is met. Footnote disclosure of such pledges is sometimes made. Unconditional pledges are recorded as assets when evidence of a binding promise is given the donee, except that colleges generally do not record pledges until paid. The assets are recorded at their estimated realizable value, which is net of an allowance for uncollectible pledges. The amount of the allowance is normally based on historical experience. The accounting literature does not specify whether pledges payable over a long period should be discounted to reflect the time value of money. In practice this is not done.

The new FASB standards require colleges to record unconditional pledges when made and require discounting to present value, with accretion of the discount being recorded as contributions income. Otherwise, there are no changes from existing standards for donees for recording the pledge asset.

As for donors, standards presently vary. Some foundations accrue grants payable; some do not. Other charitable donors generally accrue allocations and awards. For-profit donors sometimes accrue unpaid pledges, but not always. The new standards require all donors to accrue unconditional pledges payable as liabilities at their present value—the same rule as for donees, except applied backwards. The recording of the donee's revenue (expense to donors) is discussed below.

There are two related judgments that must be made in deciding whether or when to record a pledge: Is there really a pledge at all (versus a vague intention to give)? If so, are there any conditions to be fulfilled before the pledge becomes binding on the donor? These judgments must be made on a case-by-case basis; there are no formal rules. Some of the factors that should be considered in determining whether a pledge exists include whether the pledge is explicitly binding, whether the donee has announced the pledge publicly and the donor has not disagreed, whether partial payment has been made, the language used in the pledge document, whether the donee has made commitments based on reliance on the pledge, and how specific the pledge is in terms of amount, payment schedule, or use of the gift. As for conditionality, one should consider the exact language of the pledge, how explicitly the condition is defined, the likelihood of the event occurring and within what time period, and the extent to which occurrence can be facilitated by action of the donee.

Because recording (or not recording) pledges can make a considerable difference in the apparent financial condition of the donee (and maybe the donor), fund raisers will find that sometimes management will very much want (or not want) to record some pledges. Especially with major fund drives and with very large single pledges, as soon as plans are made or evidence of the pledge becomes apparent, the fund raiser is well advised to discuss with management of the donee, and with the donor, whether either has concerns about the way the pledge is to be accounted for. The fund raiser should be familiar with the different methods of accounting and the factors used in deciding which method is proper so that all alternatives can be discussed. For example, maybe both the donor and donee do not wish to record the pledge until a later period. In that case, if both agree, the language of the pledge can be written to make the pledge nonbinding or to include a condition that will not be met until the later period. Of course, there will be times in any fund raiser's career when one party wants to record the pledge and the other does not. Since the rules are the same for both, one of them will have to be flexible; maybe some inducement by one will convince the other. The fund raiser may be able to close the deal by facilitating such negotiation.

Bequests are special kinds of pledges in that they are often not made known to the donee until long after they are "made" (that is, written into a will). In general, bequests should not be recorded until the will has been probated and the court has given the executor authority to distribute the estate, because of the uncertainty as to whether there will be enough assets remaining after taxes, debts, expenses, and claims of other heirs to pay the bequest. (If the bequest is a specific one of modest size from a much larger estate and it appears very likely that the amount will be received, it would be appropriate to record this when the donor dies.)

Revenue and restricted gifts

Even more important than when pledges are recorded as assets is when all gifts, including pledges, are recorded as revenue. This is because readers of financial statements usually pay more attention to the relationships among revenues, expenses, and fund balance (net assets) than they do to noncash assets (for discussion of the uses of such data, see Lindahl, this volume; Weber, this volume).

The question of when revenue should be recorded is challenging. Presently, at least four different methods are used for different kinds of gifts to different kinds of donees. The determining factors are the type of organization, whether the gift is explicitly restricted by the donor, what kind of restriction exists, and whether the gift is in the form of a pledge. Briefly, the accounting literature specifies that explicitly time-restricted gifts ("for your 199X program") are revenue in the specified period; pledges are revenue in the period specified for payment (or if none is specified, then when paid); gifts restricted for a particular operating purpose ("for cancer research") are revenue: to a charity when received, to a college or a health care provider when the specific gift is spent, and to all other types of not-for-profits (those covered by the AICPA's Statement of Position 78–10) when any money is spent in meeting the restriction; unrestricted and endowment gifts are revenue when received. Practices relating to split-interest (deferred) gifts are complex and varied and are discussed later.

The new standard is that all unconditional gifts (including pledges) will be revenue when the gift or pledge is first received; a prepayment of a conditional pledge is still revenue only when the condition is met. The effect of this new standard will be that many not-for-profits will record some of their revenue sooner than they do now. This means usually higher revenue, larger excess of revenue over expenses, and larger fund balances. These organizations will appear to be in better financial condition than heretofore and thus will sometimes present fund raisers with the additional challenge of convincing prospective donors that new gifts are truly needed. Fund raisers will need to be adept at pointing out to donors that parts of the resources of the donee are legally restricted and cannot be used for general operations.

Heretofore, not-for-profits have reported revenue and fund balances by funds: current unrestricted, current restricted, plant (fixed asset), endowment, and sometimes others. The new standards call for only three "classes": unrestricted, or resources with no donor-imposed restriction; temporarily restricted, or resources with a donor-imposed restriction that lapses with the passage of time or is fulfilled by action of the donee; and permanently restricted, or resources with a donor-imposed restriction that never lapses or is never fulfilled.

Included in the unrestricted class will be all board-designated funds (quasi-endowment, for special projects, or other purposes) and property, plant, and equipment purchased with unrestricted resources. The temporarily restricted class will comprise operating restricted funds, term endowments, annuity and life income (split-interest) funds, unspent gifts restricted for acquisition of fixed assets, and fixed assets donated or acquired with funds restricted for that purpose. Pledges payable in a future period are considered implicitly time-restricted until that period. In the permanently restricted class will be permanent endowment and revolving loan funds.

Fund raisers soliciting unrestricted gifts will call donors' attention to the financial data for the unrestricted class, and similarly for other types of gifts. A donee may have a large endowment or other restricted balance but still be genuinely in need of unrestricted gifts because the restricted resources are not available except for specific purposes. Fund raisers should not, however, attempt to gloss over quasi-endowment funds and mislead donors into believing that these cannot be spent. Quasi endowments are legally unrestricted and thus can be spent at any time with approval of the board of the organization. Some boards may wish to pretend that they cannot use quasi endowments, but since that is not the case, there is a risk of losing credibility with donors.

The main conceptual issue involved with classifying revenue is that of determining whether there is truly a donor-imposed restriction on a gift. This, too, is often a matter of judgment and may call for an interpretation of the donor's intent by the donor or by an attorney. Some of the factors to be considered include the exact language used by the donor, whether refund of unspent amounts is called for, the presence of nonprogrammatic "compliance" requirements, and the donee's intent in soliciting the gift.

As with pledges, the fund raiser may be able to work with the donor to structure a gift so that accounting for it does not have adverse side effects for the donee. (In this case, the method of recording by the donee does not affect the accounting by the donor.) For example, a charity may receive support from a federated fundraising organization whose policy is to deduct any unrestricted surplus as of year's end from the following year's allocation. An unexpected unrestricted gift received just before year's end can result in a surplus; the gift in effect ends up being turned over to the other funder next year. However, if approached with a proposal to restrict the gift to some specific anticipated need of the donee, the donor may be willing to comply, thereby retaining the gift for the charity. Fund raisers must always be up-to-date on the entire fundraising and financial picture of an organization, and alert for opportunities to plan gifts to achieve maximum benefit for both parties.

Another accounting issue of concern to fund raisers is when and how program expenses paid with restricted gifts are reported and how these expenses are "matched" in the financial statements with that revenue. Current principles are that when restricted resources are available for a particular activity, and money is spent to conduct that activity, it is presumed that the restricted resources were used, even though the entity may also have unrestricted resources available and may even have specifically used money identified as unrestricted. In the latter case, the restricted resources that remain are then considered unrestricted, by virtue of the donor's restriction having been fulfilled. An exception to all of this is that colleges presently have the option of specifying whether the resources used were unrestricted or restricted. FASB's new standards specify that restricted resources are always deemed to have been used first, thus removing the present flexibility enjoyed by colleges to "hold back" restricted gifts for future use even while fulfilling the donors' restrictions with other money.

An additional aspect of reporting program expenses is where they are shown in the statement of revenue and expenses. Under existing practices, expenses financed with restricted resources are reported in the restricted fund. FASB's new requirement is to report all expenses in the unrestricted class, with restricted resources being reclassified (transferred) to the unrestricted class to match the expenses incurred. Fund raisers will now have to be prepared to explain to donors how the donee reports the use of their gifts: At first, it will look like no restricted gifts have been used. Since all expenses will be in the unrestricted class, the restricted class will show no expenses, which some donors will question. Also in computing the ratio of program expenses to contributions (an indicator used by some to evaluate a donee's performance), fund raisers will take the program expense number from the unrestricted class but have to add together unrestricted and restricted gifts to obtain the denominator of the ratio.

Split-interest gifts

This category refers to the several types of gift arrangements involving "split" interests, that is, both the donor and the donee receive benefits, at least for a while. The task of accounting for the five stages in the life of a split-interest gift (initial receipt; periodic income; periodic payments to life tenant; periodic actuarial revaluation of remainder interest, if applicable; and final distribution of corpus) is not well defined in accounting literature. Further, accounting for different types of gifts varies with the exact gift arrangement, and sometimes with different types of organizations. Hence, a wide variety of methods is used in practice.

Space does not permit a full discussion of all of the accounting issues for these gifts, but fund raisers should be aware of which methods are used by an organization. If a type of gift not previously received by an organization appears in prospect, the fund raiser should discuss the proposed accounting with the organization's chief financial officer and, maybe, its independent auditor so that appropriate information can be communicated to the donor if requested. Further, because tax attributes of these gifts are complex, and significant to the donor, the fund raiser should be certain that donors are receiving adequate professional advice prior to making these gifts.

Briefly, the accounting issues are as follows: Is the initial receipt of the gift recorded as revenue, deferred revenue, or an addition to the fund balance? Is the initial amount discounted to present value? Are the annual income and the payments to the life tenant recorded as revenue and expense of the donee? How is any actuarial adjustment presented? And how is the final distribution presented in the donee's financial statements? The answers to these questions are relevant in determining how to assess the performance of the organization in soliciting and managing these gifts.

Noncash gifts and donor tax deductions

This section discusses issues related to the recording of gifts that are not in the form of cash or marketable securities. These gifts include gifts of assets (real estate, equipment, supplies, collectibles, and non-marketable investments), donated services of volunteers, and the use of property. The two questions here are, Should the gift be recorded at all and, if so, at what amount?

Generally, gifts of assets are recorded at their estimated fair value, which is theoretically the amount the donee would have had to pay on the open market to acquire items of similar utility. Fair value can be determined by an appraisal, reference to sellers' catalogues or price lists, recent purchase prices of similar items, or other sources. Items sold shortly after receipt are usually recorded at the selling price. (In certain circumstances, sale of an asset by the donee can affect the allowable tax deduction by the donor.) Certain assets are not always recorded: gifts of emergency supplies to disaster relief agencies, because of the logistical problems of counting, valuing, and tracking large quantities of diverse and difficult-to-value items such as used clothing under disaster conditions, and museum collection objects, because of the difficulty in determining meaningful values for many items, and the unique status of such objects (usually retained indefinitely and not directly income producing; see also the next section on pass-through gifts).

Fund raisers soliciting such gifts should be aware of what the donee's policies are about accounting for them, in case donors inquire. Sometimes the donor will ask what value the donee is placing on a gift. Usually the donor is looking for support for the tax deduction to be taken. While a donee may choose to satisfy a donor's pure curiosity, the donee should, under no circumstances, assume the role of an appraiser for the donor. In fact, for gifts valued over $5,000, the tax code forbids a donee from appraising such gifts. It is the donor's responsibility to obtain an independent appraisal for tax purposes. The donee does not wish to become involved in a possible later dispute between the donor and the Internal Revenue Service (IRS) over the proper value of the property.

For gifts over $500, the donor must complete IRS Form 8283 and attach it to the tax return. If the gift is over $5,000, the donee will be asked to sign the form; this signature merely acknowledges receipt of the items and in no way attests to their value. If the donor appears to misunderstand this, the donee should so inform the donor. Further, if the donor does not appear to be aware of the requirement to file Form 8283, the donee should advise the donor of this. Both of these pieces of advice will likely avoid later donor unhappiness, which, were it to occur, would certainly reduce the likelihood of future gifts. Finally, if the donee sells an item within two years of receipt, the donee must advise the IRS (and the donor), on Form 8282, of the amount received from the sale. Donees are well advised to warn donors of this requirement. The donee does not want a donor who overvalues the amount of a deduction to blame the donee for a personal tax audit that is triggered by a report of a later sale of the item for a much lower amount.

Accounting for donated services of volunteers and the use of property is another area of controversy. Some accountants argue that no value should be recorded; some believe that it is appropriate to record such contributions. Arguments against recording usually focus on (1) the fact that there is (in most cases) no effect on the excess of revenues over expenses or on the fund balance because recording these items usually involves recording equal amounts of revenue and expenses (an exception is when the volunteers create a capitalizable asset such as a building), (2) the fact that no cash changes (or ever will change) hands, and (3) the alleged unnecessary effort required to track the hours worked by volunteers and assign a value to them. Arguments for recording are that the effort to track and value volunteers' hours is not that great and, mainly, that failure to record these contributions and related expense understates the extent to which the organization has been the beneficiary of public support, and the extent to which the organization has utilized available resources (including volunteers) in performing its activities. I concur with these latter points.

The accounting literature is not very definitive, and practice varies widely. There is an understandable, but not defensible, tendency to be more desirous of recording a value for volunteers who are performing program functions than for those working in administration or fundraising. In fact, fundraising volunteers are rarely recorded for two other reasons: Many of them often work more or less on their own and thus are not under the degree of supervision that allows easy tracking of time worked, and an objective determination of a value to assign per hour is usually not possible, due to the lack of comparable paid work. Another category of volunteer almost never recorded, for the same reasons, is the board member.

FASB's new requirements standardize accounting for volunteer services by means of two criteria that, if either is met, require recording; if neither criterion is met, recording would be barred. (Disclosure in a note added to the financial statements of unrecorded contributed services will be encouraged.) The two criteria are as follows: (1) if the services create or enhance nonfinancial assets and (2) if the services require specialized skills, are performed by persons possessing those skills, and would otherwise have to be purchased by the recipient if volunteers were not available. The definition of specialized skills remains to be worked out, and the determination of whether the organization would have otherwise paid someone to perform the services will require judgment in each situation. The services will be valued in the first case by the value of the asset (less any purchased components), and in the second case by the amount the provider did not charge (which such persons can easily state).

One nonaccounting question is often raised by volunteers: Can the volunteer take a personal tax deduction for the value of the time spent? The answer is unequivocally no, per Income Tax Regulation 1.170A-1(g). Volunteers can deduct certain out-of-pocket expenditures incidental to their work as volunteers.

Fund raisers should be aware that all of the rules defining amounts deductible by donors are complex, and donors should consult their own tax advisers for guidance. Fund raisers should not, unless they are professionally qualified in this area, give tax advice to donors. This has a high probability of leading to trouble later. Areas in which the rules are especially complicated, and fund raisers should warn donors to seek competent advice, include all noncash gifts, especially gifts of inventory by businesses, gifts of life insurance, and gifts of appreciated property; gifts to recipients that are classified as private foundations; gifts that constitute a significant percentage of the donor's income for the year; gifts that are bargain sales; gifts payable over several years;

bequests; gifts of a partial interest in property (including the split-interest arrangements discussed earlier); and gifts for use outside the United States.

Pass-through gifts

Several related accounting issues come into play whenever the simple donor-donee relationship is expanded to include one or more additional parties. The additional party could be a charitable entity whose purpose is to solicit gifts for another organization, or any organization that holds and manages assets for the benefit of an operating not-for-profit entity.

Some not-for-profits establish "captive" or controlled affiliates to either solicit gifts or hold assets; others participate in noncontrolled federated fundraising organizations such as United Way. Some donors give donations to independent third parties such as a bank trust department or a community foundation with instructions to invest the assets and pay the income to specified charitable beneficiaries. In many cases the trustee may not invade the principal of the gift, but in some cases the trustee has discretion about such invasion.

Whenever a not-for-profit establishes a controlled affiliate, a determination is required as to whether the affiliate should be combined with the "parent" for purposes of the parent's financial statements. A parallel determination is whether, in separate financial statements of the affiliate (if prepared), any gifts made to it are properly reported as its revenue or whether such gifts are merely amounts held on behalf of the parent, and not revenue of the affiliate. Such amounts held are reported on the balance sheet as liabilities.

These determinations depend on an assessment of how much control is exercised by the parent over the governance, management, and activities of the affiliate. If the control is very strong, the affiliate should be combined into the parent's financial statements, and in separate statements the affiliate should report gifts to it as amounts held, not as revenue. If control is very weak, the affiliate need not be combined, and gifts to it are reported as its revenue (and later reported as grant expense when remitted to the parent). A great deal of judgment is required to decide whether the level of control is high enough to qualify as strong. The accounting literature is not very well defined on this issue; practice is diverse (although in cases where a related party is not combined, disclosure of the existence of and nature of transactions with the related party is required). AICPA has issued an exposure draft of new standards (AICPA, 1993b), and FASB is also working on improving the usefulness of standards in this area.

Factors that should be considered in assessing the strength of control include the degree of overlap of governing boards and management; relevant provisions of governing documents, contractual or other agreements; the extent of required review and approval of the actions of one entity by the other; and the impression given to outsiders by the organizations' fundraising material and annual reports. The last factor is important: When a donor gives to the affiliate, does the donor think of it as really a gift to the parent? If so, there is likely strong control.

When assets functioning as endowment are held by an independent third party, the charitable beneficiary of the income normally does not include such assets on its balance sheet. If the trustee has discretion as to when and in what amounts to pay income to the charity, the charity records such amounts as contributions when received. If the trustee has no discretion but must pay over all income as received, the charity records this as investment income.

In both of the above situations, the charity's receipt of income from the third-party trustee distorts certain normal relationships among financial statement data. In one case, contributions, but not related fundraising expenses, are reported by the charity; in the other, investment income is reported, but the underlying assets are not shown. Thus, persons seeking to analyze financial data for organizations where certain activities are carried out by other entities must consider the impact of any of the accounting practices just described on the data being analyzed, as "expected" relationships will often not be observed. Specifically, fund raisers will find that evaluation of the fundraising efficiency for such organizations requires more than merely dividing reported fundraising expenses by reported contributions.

Auditing and internal accounting controls

These subjects, well covered in other literature, are mentioned briefly here to reinforce their importance. Primary responsibility for establishing sound controls and arranging for audits usually belongs to the organization's accounting staff, not the fund raiser. However, these matters are of concern to the fund raiser because of the close relationship among the functions of raising, controlling, and auditing gifts. If the fund raiser senses a lax attitude of management or the accounting staff about these matters, he or she is well advised to bring the problem to the attention of someone in the organization. Not only can weak controls lead to a loss of assets by the organization, but also publicity about instances of loss will hurt the fund raiser's ability to attract gifts.

Contributions to charities are inherently the most difficult of all types of accounting transactions over which to establish strong internal controls and a thorough audit process. This is due to the nonreciprocal nature of the transaction: Cash comes in but no goods or services are provided in exchange. Thus, many of the checks and balances used in businesses or control sales and cash receipts are not available to a charity. This means that while management personnel should try to establish as strong a control environment as possible, the challenge to do so is great, and they must always be alert to weaknesses that could allow misappropriation of assets.

Accounting for fundraising expenses

Reported fundraising expenses figure prominently in many assessments of the efficiency and effectiveness of fundraising efforts and of the charity overall. Whether this is really good or bad is left to others to discuss, although I believe that too much importance is often ascribed to fundraising expenses. Nevertheless, fund raisers must understand them to be able to discuss them intelligently.

Fundraising expenses are those expenses incurred to induce donors to contribute to an organization. Such expenses must be reported separately in the financial statements of organizations that solicit significant amounts of gifts from the general public. The new FASB standards will require such disclosure by all not-for-profits (except where these costs are immaterial to an entity). Issues relating to these expenses include what types of expenses should be called fundraising, when they should be reported as expenses, and when and how to allocate multiple-purpose expenses.

Expenses that are fundraising

The short definition given above requires elaboration to fully describe all of the various types of activities comprehended. These include planning fundraising campaigns, managing the fundraising process, actual public solicitation costs (mail, media, and so on), applying for foundation and government grants, training and supervising fundraising volunteers, staff time required to participate in federated fundraising campaigns, and other costs intended to advance the solicitation effort.

Some costs are usually not changed to fundraising, such as accounting for contributions received, which is considered an administrative cost. Some consider the cost of recruitment of all volunteers to be a fundraising expense, others consider it an administrative expense (akin to hiring paid staff), and still others would have the cost follow the duties of the volunteers being recruited. The accounting literature does not speak to this point, and practice varies; so if such costs are significant, financial statement users should inquire as to which method is followed.

The subject of recording a value for the time of fundraising volunteers was mentioned earlier in the discussion of noncash gifts. Generally, as noted, such values are not recorded. Thus, comparison of fundraising efficiency between two charities, one of which relies heavily on volunteers for fundraising and the other of which uses paid staff, is not very meaningful (see also the earlier section on pass-through gifts for a discussion of fundraising cost issues related to such gifts).

One other category of costs related to fundraising is usually not reported as fundraising expense: costs directly benefiting participants in "special events" such as dinners, parties, games, athletic activities, and sales of items such as cookies and greeting cards. For example, at a dinner, costs of food, decorations, entertainment, and prizes are for items that benefit attendees, not the organization. On the other hand, costs of invitations, planning, and publicity do not directly benefit attendees. Costs benefiting attendees are reported as an offset to revenue from the event, other costs are fundraising. So if one pays $500 a plate to attend a dinner and the costs to the organization of putting it on are $65 for food and entertainment and $20 for publicity, the financial statements would show $500 of gross revenue less $65 direct costs for net revenue of $435, and fundraising expenses of $20.

Two tax matters should be noted here: If the attendee could have purchased a comparable dinner for, say, $100, the tax deduction available is $400 ($500 payment less $100 value received); and in the IRS Form 990 filed by the organization, it will report $400 of the ticket price as a contribution (line 1) and $100 as proceeds from special fundraising events (line 9a). The $65 is shown as an offset to the $100 (line 9b), and the $20 as fundraising expense (line 15). Fund raisers should have at least a basic understanding of these tax matters, especially those that affect donors' deductions. Further, the organization must advise donors who receive an item of significant value in return for a donation (dinner, books or records, and so on) of the portion of their payment that is not tax deductible; failure to do so (or the use of vague phrases such as "Your gift is deductible to the extent provided by law") can attract an IRS penalty.

When to report fundraising expenses

Although fundraising costs incurred in one period often result in contributions received in future periods, accountants generally require that these costs be expensed in the period incurred rather than partly deferred to future periods. This requirement is due largely to the inherent uncertainty of the response to any fundraising activity, which leads to an inability to accurately assess the extent to which such expenses actually have any remaining value at the end of the year in which they were incurred. Even expenses incurred in one year to develop long-range giving programs, such as capital campaigns or deferred (split-interest) gifts and bequests, must be reported as expenses when incurred, not deferred until gifts are received. (One exception to this rule is that unused supplies of printed materials can be carried as inventories, so long as they are reasonably expected to be used in future periods.) Thus, comparison of fundraising expenses reported in one accounting period with contributions reported in the same period may or may not accurately reflect the real cause-and-effect relationship of these items.

Currently, a project is under way at AICPA regarding accounting for advertising costs for businesses. In the past, such costs have also been expensed when incurred. AICPA is proposing to allow deferral of costs of soliciting so-called direct-response advertising (solicitation of mail or telephone orders) when a historical relationship can be demonstrated between such costs incurred in one period and sales in a subsequent period, which the nature of direct-response advertising makes possible. Although this advertising project explicitly excludes fundraising efforts of not-for-profits, the parallel with fundraising is so obvious that consideration may be given to extending the principle at some later date.

Allocation of expenses

The general question of allocation arises whenever an expense benefits more than one activity. For example if office space is shared by two departments, the monthly rent is allocated to the departments, usually on the basis of amount of space occupied. Similar allocations are often required for salaries, utilities, supplies, and other expenses. In most cases, the basis of allocation can be readily determined: salaries by time spent, supplies by usage, or occupancy by space occupied. The allocation process does require additional record keeping: time sheets or effort reports by personnel, estimates of supply usage, or computation of space occupied. Then work sheet calculations produce the allocated amounts.

Once total fundraising costs are determined, by adding directly charged and allocated amounts, it may be desired to subdivide these costs into components representing the costs of each separate fundraising activity, for example, various separate mailings, television advertisements, door-to-door, and solicitation of grants. The process is the same as before; however, the smaller the final pieces, the more difficult it becomes to be objective about the allocations, and the less precise the outcome. That is, in attempting to subdivide fundraising expenses, one must recognize that the result does not have the same level of accuracy as achieved with larger-scale amounts.

One particular allocation problem requires separate discussion: allocation of "joint" costs. These occur when a cost item simultaneously benefits more than one function and there is no objective method available to decide how much of the cost to allocate to each function. In fundraising, this situation most often occurs with multiple-purpose mailings, such as those containing both educational material (for example, the seven warning signs of cancer) and an appeal for donations. The printing costs of each component are not at issue here; those are charged directly to the respective function. The issue is the joint costs: the outside envelope, mailing list rental, staff time to coordinate the mailing, and (usually the largest item) postage.

Two questions must be answered: Is it at all appropriate to allocate the joint costs and, if so, on what basis? These questions may seem trivial, but they are not. If it were always true that such mailings had a bona fide educational purpose, then the question of whether to allocate would be moot. However, often such mailings are really just solicitations, and any educational component is an afterthought, added to take advantage of the mailing going out anyway. How does one distinguish the genuine program activity? State charity regulators are especially concerned about this issue (see Ormstedt, this volume).

The accounting profession has published guidance in AICPA (1987), *Accounting for Joint Costs of Informational Materials and Activities of Not-for-Profit Organizations That Include a Fund-Raising Appeal.* (AICPA [1993a] has produced a new statement that amplifies and clarifies but does not change the basic premises of the 1987 document.) This standard defines several requirements that must all be met in order to allocate joint costs to functions other than fundraising. These requirements are as follows: (1) there must be verifiable evidence of the reasons for conducting the activity, (2) the content of the activity must include a bona fide purpose other than fundraising, (3) the audience targeted must have a legitimate interest in the non–fundraising component of the activity, and (4) the non–fundraising component must include material designed to motivate its audience to action other than contributing to the organization.

Clearly, professional judgment is required in deciding whether these requirements are met. The first requirement is judged partly on the answers to the other three, as well as on criteria such as written management plans and board resolutions, and assignment of overall responsibility for the activity to persons other than fund raisers. The second requirement is judged on the inherent value of the material and its consistency with the stated purposes of the organization. The third requirement has two components: the assumed wealth of the audience (as measured by income statistics for the geographical areas targeted, under the assumption that a wealthier audience is more likely to have been targeted for its fundraising potential) and the presumed benefit to the audience of receiving the information (measured by data such as epidemiological statistics for a disease, demographic data, or other methods). The fourth requirement is best illustrated by an example. If the "educational" material merely described the seven warning signs of cancer, that would not count. It must say, "Here are the seven warning signs of cancer; if you notice any of them, *go* to your doctor." The action is "go to your doctor." The presumption is that learning about something is of real value only when one takes beneficial action based on that knowledge. The action called for must be fairly specific: "Don't pollute" is too vague, but "Don't dump used motor oil in a storm drain" would qualify. The action may benefit the person receiving the message, or it could also benefit other people ("Don't drink and drive") or the environment (the motor oil example).

When working with a charity to plan a fundraising activity that will include an educational component, fund raisers should be aware of these requirements so they can help the charity comply with the accounting rules if allocation of some of the costs to program activities is desired.

The second allocation question is what and how to allocate. What to allocate was discussed earlier; how is often a difficult question. It might seem that one could merely measure the relative quantities of educational versus fundraising material (lines of print, square units of space, or some comparable measure). However, first, not all material is of equal value: How does one count photographs, for example, or blank space used for emphasis of surrounding material, or various sizes of type, or sweepstakes tickets? Second, if relative quantity were the sole measure, charities attempting to minimize fundraising costs would simply use the technique well known to writers of school term papers: padding. Educational material would expand to fit the desired outcome, likely with little or no additional benefit to readers; in fact, the benefit might decrease as the message drowns in a sea of fluff. As a result, judgment is significant to the question of how to allocate. Certainly, content can be considered, but so too the relative impact and usefulness of the material, the apparent intent of the activity, the need of the audience for the educational material, and other relevant factors.

Assessing fundraising efficiency

Although this subject is not an accounting matter, it does depend partly on accounting data. What I have shown here is that the use of accounting data to help assess fundraising efficiency must be done carefully, due to the interaction of various accounting principles that determine when and how contributions and fundraising expenses are reported in financial statements.

Other tax considerations

Besides the various tax matters discussed earlier in this chapter, one more is of concern to fund raisers: private foundation status. The subject does not come up often, but when it does, the consequences can be severe for both donor and donee. Thus, fund raisers should know enough to recognize a potential problem and seek professional advice.

Briefly, all organizations exempt from tax under Internal Revenue

Code Section 501(c)(3) (the section that covers most entities to which tax-deductible gifts may be made) are either private foundations or public charities. Public charity status is much more desirable for both the charity and its donors, since private foundation status imposes a number of rather onerous constraints on the charity as well as limits the amount of tax deduction available to donors in some cases.

The determination of whether an organization is considered a private foundation is based to a great extent on from whom and in what amounts contributions are received. Thus, when soliciting gifts for a charity, fund raisers must be conscious of what types of gifts could include a risk of the charity being reclassified as a private foundation as a result of the gift. (Tax specialists use the word *tipping* to refer to this occurrence: The public charity is tipped into private foundation status.) Or, if the organization is already a private foundation, the fund raiser should be sure that prospective donors are aware of that fact and its consequences to them. (It is not within the scope of this chapter, or normally within the professional competence of the fund raiser, to discuss these consequences. Donors should obtain their own tax advice.)

The types of gifts that can lead to private foundation status are basically any large gift from an individual, company, or private foundation and any gift from so-called disqualified persons: officers, directors, and trustees of the charity, their relatives, and businesses with which they are associated, and previous donors of large gifts. (The definitions of these types of gifts are complex and the exact language of the Internal Revenue Code, in Section 509(a), should be consulted.) While a fund raiser may seek such gifts, he or she should do so with an awareness of the tax rules and of when additional professional advice is needed.

References

American Institute of Certified Public Accountants (AICPA). *Accounting Principles and Reporting Practices for Certain Nonprofit Organizations.* Statement of Position No. 78-10. New York: AICPA, 1978.

American Institute of Certified Public Accountants. *Accounting for Joint Costs of Informational Materials and Activities of Not-for-Profit Organizations That Include a Fund-Raising Appeal.* Statement of Position No. 87-2. New York: AICPA, 1987.

American Institute of Certified Public Accountants. *Accounting for Costs of Materials and Activities of Not-for-Profit Organizations and State and Local Governmental Entities That Include a Fund-Raising Appeal.* (Exposure drafts). New York: AICPA, 1993a.

American Institute of Certified Public Accountants. *Reporting of Related Entities by Not-for-Profit Organizations.* New York: AICPA, 1993b.

Financial Accounting Standards Board (FASB). *Accounting for Contributions Received and Contributions Made.* Statement of Financial Accounting Standards No. 116. Norwalk, Conn.: FASB, 1993a.

Financial Accounting Standards Board. *Financial Statements of Not-for-Profit Organizations.* Statement of Financial Accounting Standards No. 117. Norwalk, Conn.: FASB, 1993b.

RICHARD F. LARKIN *is national technical director of the Not-for-Profit Industry Services Group of Price Waterhouse, Bethesda, Maryland, and a member of the Not-for-Profit Advisory Task Force of the Financial Accounting Standards Board.*

A case is made for the practical utility of audits and measurements to demonstrate the productivity and efficiency and the cost-effectiveness and profitability of fundraising.

3

Criteria for audits and measurements for demonstrating fundraising success

Arthur S. Collier

SCARCITY OF AND COMPETITION for financial resources in the nonprofit sector and philanthropic world have alerted board members, volunteers, donors, and others to the need for performance measurements, resulting in greater accountability. Fundraising professionals who are successful in the 1990s will utilize new economic tools to demonstrate the productivity and effectiveness of their resource development programs. In this regard, there are three fundamental questions: Why are new economic tools vital to success? What new economic tools will be needed and what criteria should be used to measure fundraising performance? By what standards should fundraising performance be evaluated?

Practical utility of audits and measurements

Why are new economic tools vital to success? The answer to this question is based on two concepts: resource development (fundraising) as a business enterprise and resource development as a public trust.

NEW DIRECTIONS FOR PHILANTHROPIC FUNDRAISING, NO. 3, SPRING 1994 © JOSSEY-BASS PUBLISHERS

Resource development as a business enterprise

As a business enterprise, resource development has three distinct features: (1) It is a *unique* business that may not work the way chief executive officers (CEOs), chief financial officers (CFOs), and board members wish, think, or believe it should work, (2) it is a *separate* business within a larger business and is totally different from the institutional business, and (3) it is in many important ways the *same* as any other business enterprise.

Resource development is unique because it has its own economics, methodologies, performance criteria, and terminology. Perhaps the most salient feature of its uniqueness is its potential for returning the highest rate of return on investment of any business enterprise within a nonprofit institution.

The role of resource development is to help nonprofit institutions carry out their missions. But resource development as a business is not in the same business as the institution that it serves. It is not in the business of education or health care or the arts or social welfare. It is in the business of fundraising. It is a separate business enterprise within the larger business enterprise of the institution.

As unique and separate as resource development may be, in some very fundamental ways it is the same as all business enterprises in that it requires planning, management, performance measurement, and financial investment. The old cliché that will not go away is that it still takes money to make money.

It is my premise that the level of financial investment and the method by which nonprofit institutions finance their development programs are the key indicators of the institution's level of readiness for and commitment to be successful in fundraising. Let us consider how institutions approach the financing of their fundraising business enterprise. There are two basic approaches.

What can we afford? The first approach, "What can we afford?" is focused only on cost, the expense of fundraising, and has the following characteristics: (1) The fundraising budget is determined in relationship to the total budget requirements of the institution and anticipated institutional revenues. (2) The fundraising budget is subject to adjustment (that is, reduction) according to institutional financial performance.

This approach does not recognize that fundraising is a separate and unique business (within the larger business) that can be highly productive at exactly the same time that the institutional business is floundering, which is the very time the institution needs an increase in revenue. When overall revenues decline, many CEOs and CFOs believe in the simplistic mandate that "everyone share the pain" of budget reductions, including the development program, regardless of its productivity. The result is almost always less revenue from fundraising.

This expense-focused approach to financial investment in fundraising does not consider the value of long-term financial stability that results from a commitment to initiate and develop new revenue-producing programs and allow them the time to achieve their financial potential. The "cash only" results prevent long-range buildup of assets that can yield added revenues through earned income. Rather than build a comprehensive interrelated resource development program that will maximize philanthropic potential from all possible constituencies, the development professional must choose among solicitation programs that will deliver cash only, the biggest "bang for the buck" in the shortest period of time.

How much can we raise? The other approach focuses on revenues rather than expenses. The question is, first, "How much money can we raise?" and then, "How much money do we have to spend to get it?" The focus is on return on investment rather than the dollars spent. This approach has the following characteristics: (1) Financial investment in staff and solicitation programs is based on potential for return. (2) Staffing levels are based on work load capacities (related to type of activity) and per capita production standards. (3) Fundraising costs by types of programs are planned and evaluated against productivity norms based on the number of years that the programs have been in development. (4) The annual financial investment for staff and program is constantly expanded as long as there is profitable performance and unrealized potential.

This approach to financing a fundraising program results in the long-term financial stability needed to build a comprehensive interrelated program that can maximize the philanthropic potential of all age groups and all socioeconomic levels from both earned income and accumulated assets through both current and deferred giving. The nonprofit institution that utilizes this investment approach is more likely to experience increased philanthropic support even when operational revenues from the institutional business are in decline.

Expense-focused dilemma. The expense-focused approach presents a twofold challenge to the fundraising professional. In the short term, he or she must determine how to use the limited financial and human resources to get the most production for the dollars spent. How can the practical utilization of audits and measurements help?

In this situation a resource development professional needs to know three things: (1) How productive and efficient are each of these short-term fundraising programs? Productivity and efficiency analysis can help answer this question. (2) Are there other areas of potential that could be more productive than the areas solicited by the current program? A market analysis and assessment of philanthropic potential from an audit or feasibility study can help answer this question. (3) How much revenue could a fundraising program produce in the first year and over five years? A program financial pro forma can help answer this question.

If the fundraising professional desires to move beyond the limitations of the expense-focused approach, he or she must then address a second challenge: how to move the institution to a revenue- and production-focused approach to financing its fundraising program. I believe that the expense-focused approach is the greatest handicap to the ability of an institution to realize its potential from philanthropy. This limitation is self-imposed and therefore can be changed. Fundraising professionals who address this challenge will be acting in the best interests of their institutions and their careers.

There are two factors that are fundamental to realizing success in this conversion. First, the resource development professional must take the initiative. Expense-focused budgeting is the corporate culture ("the way we do things") in most nonprofit institutions. The board, CEO, and CFO are not likely to initiate alternative approaches to the way they normally manage the larger business enterprise. Second, the development professional must provide an overwhelmingly convincing and credible case that this productivity-revenue approach (exception to the practice) will help address institutional financial problems in a positive way.

The means to develop this case is found in the practical utility of audits and measurements. Assessments of new-program potential together with a clear analysis of the productivity and efficiency of current fundraising programs will encourage confidence in the fundraising enterprise. These tools will be instrumental in providing a rationale for financing fundraising in a different manner.

Never-ending challenge. Those resource development professionals who are fortunate to work for institutions that finance development programs based on productivity and return on investment must remain vigilant. There is always competition for scarce budget dollars. There always seem to be board members, rival internal enterprises, or someone who thinks development has too large a staff and spends too much money. And, administrations change.

Productivity and efficiency analysis that demonstrates all of the value of the development programs and staff is a valuable tool for maintaining this commitment to financial investment. Assessments of potential and program financial pro forma are valuable tools in efforts to expand current programs and to add new programs. Again, we see the practicality of audits and measurements.

Resource development as a public trust

Public confidence is essential to successful fundraising. Prudent stewardship of funds raised is essential to public confidence. Stewardship can best be exhibited by full and accurate disclosure of fundraising costs and productivity ratios. "How much of my contribution is actually used for the purpose I intend?" This is a question of fundraising productivity and efficiency that cannot be answered by accounting data and financial reports alone.

Larkin (this volume) provides a comprehensive overview of accounting issues that relate to fundraising. He thoroughly explains the new accounting rules for reporting contributions and accounting for fundraising expenses. He concludes, however, that assessment of fundraising productivity and efficiency (cost per dollar raised) is not an accounting matter, but it does depend partly on accounting data.

Only through productivity analysis can true costs per dollar raised be determined. Regular financial reports do not relate total production in a specific time frame to the actual expenses incurred in the same time frame to produce the dollars, regardless of when they will be received. Simply dividing all recorded fundraising revenue by all recorded fundraising expense ("bottom-line" analysis) will not result in an accurate productivity ratio.

One case in point is bequest and trust income received in the current period that is not related to planned giving expenses for the current period. Deferred income from new planned gifts completed in the current period (whether booked or not) will not show up on the operating statement, but the expenses to complete these gifts are reported. Another example is the restricted gifts that are not recognized as revenue on the operations statement when they are received, but rather when the gift is actually spent to fulfill the restricted purpose. The full cost related to raising these gifts, however, are expended on the operations statement in the current period, rather than deferred to the period in which the revenues are recognized. Another case in point is that most institutions receive unsolicited gifts (usually unrestricted) that are the result of historical relationships and not connected to any current fundraising activity. Crediting these gifts against current fundraising expenses also produces a misleading productivity ratio. Because financial statements are not designed to produce productivity ratios, attempts to use standard financial reports for this purpose usually result in the appearance of inflated costs per dollar raised.

It is now becoming apparent that fundraising productivity and efficiency affect donor choice in giving. Voluntary open and full disclosure is essential to continued public confidence and requires the use of relevant audits and measurements. The problem with public evaluation of productivity data is that there are no standardized guidelines for uniformly calculating the cost per dollar raised, nor are there recognized standards for comparing results. The latest editions of the American Institute of Certified Public Accountants audit guides for nonprofit institutions have taken large steps forward in defining uniform accounting for all types of gifts and for calculating fundraising expenses. They have not yet provided a method of relating gift revenues (whenever received) to the actual expenses incurred to produce the gifts. The Financial Accounting Standards Board is attempting to clarify these issues. Ideally, in time, a universal guideline will be developed and used to produce equitable fundraising productivity ratios in a manner that donors can understand and use. In the absence of any uniform procedures promulgated by a recognized authority, fundraising professionals must take the lead and engage their institutions in developing their own methodologies and standards of performance, not only for institutional accountability to the public but also for institutional evaluation of the fundraising business enterprise. The practical utilization of audits and measurements is a valuable, even essential, means of understanding and improving resource development as a business enterprise and a public trust.

Criteria for audits and measurements

What new economic tools are needed and what criteria should be used to measure fundraising performance? Fundraising professionals and nonprofit institutions need to study fundraising productivity and efficiency in order to address the issues of fundraising as a business based on return on investment, and fundraising as a public trust based on cost per dollar raised.

They need to supplement their financial reports with both productivity reports and efficiency reports that can be compared to industry performance standards. Productivity is a measurement of the financial results from fundraising programs, and efficiency is a statistical measurement of the activities undertaken to produce the financial results. Performance comparisons are relative measurements of productivity and efficiency.

In addition to the measurements of current activity, I suggest, based on my assessment of fundraising as a business, that fundraising professionals and nonprofit institutions also need to develop statistically based measurements of future potential. Criteria must be established for productivity reports, efficiency reports, forecasts of future philanthropic income, and performance standards.

Productivity reports

The purpose of the productivity report is to justify the current investment in fundraising, and to provide fair and accurate information to meet the public trust. Criteria for developing these productivity reports have two dimensions: identification of financial information to be included and formulas for using the information to determine productivity.

Identification of financial information. One important distinction was established earlier: Productivity reports are not the same as financial reports. A productivity report relates revenues received to the actual expenses incurred to produce that revenue, regardless of when and where the money is actually entered into the financial records. Most fundraising enterprises receive revenue from two basic sources: contributions directly related to the current efforts and costs of the fundraising programs and contributions related to past efforts and relationships that are unrelated to current efforts and costs. Productivity reports should first be concerned with the first category of revenues and expenses.

Accurate productivity ratios require that both income and expenses be properly allocated and related. Expenses should include direct program costs, indirect costs for whatever portion of salaries and benefits relate to the staff time expended on the programs, and allocated costs for space, office supplies, equipment, utilities, and support, and for management supervision and support (see Larkin, this volume, for a thorough discussion of these fundraising expenses).

The following revenues and their related expenses *should not* be included in the productivity analysis: (1) "Over-the-transom" contributions that did not require any effort or acquisition expense. The cost of processing these gifts should be isolated and removed from the analysis. (2) Payments on pledges already counted as production in a prior period. To include these is to engage in "double-dipping," resulting in inaccurate productivity ratios. Any current expense for processing these revenues should also be eliminated. (3) Current bequests and charitable remainder trust income. In most cases, the expenses to develop planned gifts in the current period have nothing to do with the receipt of matured gifts executed years before. Any expenses related to these revenues that happen to be received in the current period should also be eliminated from the productivity analysis.

The following revenues and related expenses *should* be included in the productivity analysis: (1) All new cash revenues received in the current period related to current fundraising programs with the expenses incurred to produce these revenues. (2) All new pledges committed during the period related to current fundraising programs with all the expenses incurred to generate the pledges. Multiyear pledges may be discounted to present value and an adjustment for uncollectible pledges (based on historical data) may be made. These calculations are institutional decisions guided by accounting pronouncements. (3) The value of new planned gifts committed during the current period with all the related expenses incurred to produce these agreements. After these three calculations of expense to revenue and production are completed, reasonably accurate and consistent productivity analysis can be accomplished.

A big question on planned gifts is what value to use. Most nonprofit institutions count the current market value of irrevocable trusts regardless of whether they are named as trustees. Revocable trusts also can be counted but should be segregated.

Some nonprofit institutions estimate the value of documented bequests. Generally, if the donor is well known to the institution and the amount of the bequest is disclosed, the full amount can be estimated. Bequests of unknown amounts or remainder interests are estimated by some institutions at their respective historical averages of bequest receipts or at a minimum amount, such as $1,000 or $5,000 each. These estimates are *not* entered on the financial statements but are recorded by the development office and included in their productivity analysis.

Institutions may adjust all of their deferred commitments to net present value to reflect the true value of the money when it is realized in the future. These are issues that each institution must resolve to perform a valid analysis of its planned giving productivity.

Productivity Formulas. Greenfield (1991) has defined four formulas for analyzing fundraising productivity to be applied to each fundraising activity (see also Greenfield and Dreves. 1993, pp. 674–677):

Percentage rate of return: Divide the number of responses by the number of solicitations.

Average gift size: Divide the total dollar amount of contributions received by the number of gifts received.

Average cost per gift: Divide the total fundraising cost by the number of gifts received.

Program cost percentage: Divide the program's total costs by the total contributions received and multiply by 100.

He added this admonition: "Overall 'bottom line' performance adds together the results of each fundraising activity and demonstrates the profitability and productivity of the total fund development program. Nonprofit organizations should be cautious about using 'bottom line' as the only measurement; by itself, it is inadequate information and can easily lead to a misunderstanding of the level of performance each individual fundraising method should be expected to achieve on its own" (Greenfield, 1991, p. 46).

Examples of productivity reports. Exhibit 3.1 illustrates one method for presenting productivity analysis. Costa (1991) collected from

Exhibit 3.1. Comparative Production Analysis
(for Each Program)

Production	Five-Year Average, 19__ to 19__	Last Year, 19__	This Year, 19__
Cash received			
Percentage increase (decrease) over previous year(s)			
Value of new pledges			
Percentage increase (decrease) over previous year(s)			
Value of new long-term deferred revenue			
Percentage increase (decrease) over previous year(s)			
Total production			
Percentage increase (decrease) over previous year(s)			
Total expenses			
Percentage increase (decrease) over previous year(s)			
Net gain (loss)			
Percentage increase (decrease) over previous year(s)			
Program Productivity			
Rate of return on investment			
Cost per dollar raised			

health care colleagues six other sample methodologies and report formats that measure productivity: (1) financial statements, (2) incorporation of goals into one-year performance reports, (3) fundraising cost-effectiveness analysis by type of activity, (4) fundraising cost-effectiveness comparison by type of activity, average gift, and cost per gift, (5) analysis of return on investment and cost per dollar raised, and (6) performance analysis. The variety of these reports illustrates that these fundraising professionals designed reports to meet *their* needs. The best way is the way that works best for any individual fund raiser.

Efficiency reports

The purpose of efficiency reports is to provide valuable information for planning and managing all current fundraising programs. Typically, the expectation is that fundraising revenue will increase each year. Revenues can be increased in four ways: ask more people (new prospects), increase the response rate of the new prospects solicited, increase the renewal rate of current donors, and increase the amount of the average gift (both acquisition and renewal). The efficiency report should provide performance information in all four areas to help determine the appropriate strategies for planning and adjusting the fundraising programs to increase revenues.

Information and formulas for efficiency reports. As with productivity reports, efficiency reports must be based on useful information and must utilize formulas appropriate for analysis of that information. Greenfield (1991, pp. 43–44) also has provided four formulas for analyzing the efficiency of the fundraising programs, utilizing the statistical information identified in the foregoing section:

Percentage of qualified prospects assigned: Divide the number of prospects that the volunteers selected by the total number in the prospect pool and multiply by 100.

Percentage of assigned prospects solicited: Divide the number of visits made by the number of assignments and multiply by 100.

Percentage of prior donors upgraded: Divide the total number of donors whose gifts increased by the total number of prior donors available and multiply by 100.

Percentage increase in number of donors: Subtract the number of donors last year from the number of donors this year, divide by last year's total, and multiply by 100.

These formulas by no means exhaust the possibilities, but they do define the fundamental characteristics of efficiency measurement.

Examples of efficiency reports. Exhibits 3.2, 3.3, and 3.4 illustrate several efficiency factors that can be analyzed for *each* fundraising program: direct mail, donor clubs, annual fund, special events, major gifts, and even planned giving. These efficiency reports offer four important types of information: (1) Analysis of the efficiency of the current fundraising program. Are we doing the right things? Are we doing them well? (2) Comparison of the current year performance to past performance. Are we doing these things better? (3) Trends that may be developing. Are there factors that must be addressed (such as fewer volunteer solicitors each year, or a continuing decline in response rates to donor acquisition mailings)? (4) Relationships between activity and production. How many solicitations must we make to renew direct-mail donors? How many solicitations must we make to produce a major gift? How many qualified prospects must we have to complete a planned gift? The data produced by the efficiency formulas, which can be presented as efficiency reports (see Exhibits 3.2, 3.3, and 3.4), will help fundraising professionals understand the reasons for an increase or decrease in fundraising production. Ideally, each fundraising program seeks to acquire new donors, renew old donors, and effectively utilize volunteers. These efficiency reports can be adapted for each fundraising program to analyze each of these key components.

Forecasts of future philanthropic income

The purposes in forecasting future philanthropic income are to set realistic goals for established and proposed new fundraising programs,

Exhibit 3.2. Fundraising Efficiency Analysis: Donor Acquisition

	Five-Year Average, 19__ to 19__	Last Year, 19__	This Year, 19__
Number of new prospects			
Number of new prospects actually solicited			
Percentage of new prospects actually solicited			
Percentage increase (decrease) over previous years			
Number of new donors			
Percentage of solicitations made to donor gifts (response rate)			
Percentage increase (decrease) over previous years			
Average gift size			
Percentage increase (decrease) over previous years			
Total contributions amount			
Percentage increase (decrease) over previous years			

Exhibit 3.3. Fundraising Efficiency Analysis:
Donor Renewal

	Five-Year Average, 19__ to 19__	Last Year, 19__	This Year, 19__
Number of donors on file at beginning of year			
Number of donors actually solicited			
Percentage increase (decrease) over previous years			
Number of renewed donors			
Percentage of solicitations made to renewed donors (response rate)			
Percentage increase (decrease) over previous years			
Average gift			
Percentage increase (decrease) over previous years			
Number of donors upgraded			
Percentage of donors upgraded			
Percentage increase (decrease) over previous years			

Exhibit 3.4. Fundraising Efficiency Analysis: Volunteer Performance

	Five-Year Average, 19__ to 19__	*Last Year, 19__*	*This Year, 19__*
Number of volunteers			
Percentage increase (decrease) over previous years			
Number of solicitations assigned			
Percentage increase (decrease) over previous years			
Number of solicitations completed			
Percentage increase (decrease) over previous years			
Number of gifts received			
Percentage increase (decrease) over previous years			
Average gift size			
Percentage increase (decrease) over previous years			

to justify requested budget investment for the coming year for both established and proposed fundraising programs, and to forecast reliable income the institution can expect from the fundraising programs. Forecasts of future philanthropic income should include potential income that is unrelated to the fundraising efforts planned for the coming year, potential income related to established fundraising that is expected to be continued, and potential income from new fundraising programs that will be developed during the coming year or years.

Forecasting potential income unrelated to current and future fundraising efforts. Income in this category usually comes from three sources: unsolicited (over-the-transom) contributions, bequests and trusts, and pledge payments. Unsolicited contributions can be charted over a number of years, and a trend line established to project estimated future income.

Generally, probated bequests require eighteen to twenty-four months to clear probate. An analysis of these bequests in probate can provide a fair estimate of the revenue that is likely to be received during the next calendar or fiscal year. The task of estimating potential revenues from charitable and other trusts and from life insurance policies is more difficult because these arrangements and values may not be known to the institution. In this case, past income from these same sources can be charted and a multiyear average established as a basis for projecting estimated revenues.

Scheduled pledge payments during the coming year can be calculated and adjusted for uncollectible sums (based on the institutions prior experience), and a fairly accurate estimate of income can be made. Exhibit 3.5 illustrates the presentation of this methodology.

Forecasting potential income related to established fundraising programs. The productivity of these programs can be charted with some precision over a number of years (utilizing a productivity report such as illustrated in Exhibit 3.1), and a trend line can be established as a basis for reliable income projections. These projections, however, should be

Exhibit 3.5. Forecast of Revenues Unrelated to Current Fundraising Efforts

	Trends and Projections	*Forecast*
Unsolicited Contributions		
Five-year average income	$	
Last year income	$	
Five-year trend: increase (decrease)	____%	
Projected increase (decrease)	____%	
19__ forecast		$
Bequests and Trusts		
Estates in probate	$	
Estimate to be received in 19__ (from probate)		$
Five-year average income received (other than probate)	$	
Last year income (other than probate)	$	
Five-year trend: increase (decrease)	____%	
Projected increase (decrease)	____%	
Estimate to be received in 19__		$
Total bequests and trusts: 19__ forecast		$
Pledges Receivable		
Pledge payments due in 19__	$	
Allowance for uncollectible sums	$	
19__ forecast		$
Forecast of Total Revenues Unrelated to Current Fundraising Efforts		$

adjusted according to a number of variables: trends (positive and negative) in fundraising efficiency (see Exhibits 3.2–3.4); changes in effort (staffing and financial investment), either increased or decreased; significant changes in the reputation and image of the institution (positive or negative) that may affect contributions in the coming years; and significant changes in the economic conditions (positive or negative) that may affect donors' ability to give. Exhibit 3.6 illustrates the presentation of this methodology.

Lindahl (this volume) discusses a variety of sophisticated economic models and methodologies for forecasting future results based on a multiyear evaluation of fundraising performance. Costa (1991, pp. 13–15) has gathered three types of methodologies and report forms for forecasting future revenues from past performance. These reports illustrate how development professionals have developed different report forms to meet their needs: (1) goals, forecasting, and short-range planning, (2) examples of TARGETED™ goals, and (3) projecting goals and preparing reports based on five-year cumulative averages.

Forecasting potential income from new fundraising programs. The methodology for developing estimates of potential net revenues from new fundraising programs utilizes estimates and formulas in the place of actual performance data. The methodology generally follows this format:

1. Number of identified prospects to be solicited
2. Estimated response rate
3. Projected number of gifts (item 1 multiplied by item 2)
4. Estimated average gift
5. Projected gross revenues (item 3 multiplied by item 4)
6. Estimated total costs
7. Projected net revenues (item 5 minus item 6)
8. Projected rate of return on investment (item 5 divided by item 6)

The credibility of this method is in the estimates and formulas that are utilized. The most reliable figures are those from comparable institutions, although fundraising performance varies even within the same types of nonprofit organizations.

Exhibit 3.6. Forecast of Revenues from Established Fundraising Programs

	Trends and Projections	*Forecast*
Annual Support Programs		
Five-year average income	$_____	
Last year income	$_____	
Five-year trend: increase (decrease)	____%	
Projected increase (decrease)	____%	
19__ forecast		$_____
Major Gifts Program		
Five-year average income	$_____	
Last year income	$_____	
Five-year trend: increase (decrease)	____%	
Projected increase (decrease)	____%	
19__ forecast		$_____
Foundation Grants		
Five-year average income	$_____	
Last year income	$_____	
Five-year trend: increase (decrease)	____%	
Projected increase (decrease)	____%	
19__ forecast		$_____
Forecast of Total Revenues from Established Programs		$_____

This methodology is used routinely in the business world to develop business plans and financial pro forma for new projects and ventures. And it is often used by direct-mail vendors to estimate revenue, expenses, and profits when proposing contracts for their services, as illustrated in Table 3.1. Why is it not used by nonprofit institutions for estimating fundraising results?

Exhibit 3.7 illustrates how revenue forecasts for a number of new programs could be presented. This example assumes that a new-donor club program and a corporate sponsorship program will be initiated during the year. Exhibit 3.8 utilizes all the methodologies discussed in this section, as well as cost estimates, to present a summary forecast of new revenue.

Performance standards

By what standards should fundraising performance be evaluated? Even after rates of return on investment, cost per dollar raised, production per full-time equivalence, and much more are presented, there is still one question usually raised by board members and CEOs. Is the performance good or bad? It is standard procedure for business enterprises to compare financial results and other key performance indicators against accepted industry performance standards. When resource development professionals do so as a routine part of their productivity analyses, they answer several important questions, which adds credibility to their reports. How does this performance compare with other like institutions? Are these costs reasonable?

Weber (this volume) argues that most currently available statistics, especially global norms, are misleading and suggests a better way to develop relevant comparative statistics. Weber thinks that development professionals need to identify peer groups and develop more relevant comparative statistics for evaluation purposes. Costa (1991, p. 23) provides a helpful list of sources for comparative statistics, including *USA Report on Giving* and *Canada Report on Giving,* published

Table 3.1. Five-Year Projection of Direct-Mail Potential

Phase	Year 1	2	3	4	5	Total
Acquisition						
Number mailed	100,000	100,000	100,000	100,000	100,000	500,000
Response rate	1%	1%	1%	1%	1%	1%
Number of new donors	1,000	1,000	1,000	1,000	1,000	5,000
Average gift	$30	$30	$30	$30	$30	$30
Gross revenue	$30,000	$30,000	$30,000	$30,000	$30,000	$150,000
Costs	$38,000	$38,000	$38,000	$38,000	$38,000	$190,000
Net revenue (expense)	($8,000)	($8,000)	($8,000)	($8,000)	($8,000)	($40,000)
Cost per donor	$8	$8	$8	$8	$8	$8
First-Year Renewal						
Donors		1,000	1,000	1,000	1,000	4,000
Response rate		60%	60%	60%	60%	60%
Number of gifts		600	600	600	600	2,400
Average gift		$40	$40	$40	$40	$40
Gross revenue		$24,000	$24,000	$24,000	$24,000	$96,000
Costs		$500	$500	$500	$500	$2,000
Net revenue (expense)		$23,500	$23,500	$23,500	$23,500	$94,000
Yield per donor		$39	$39	$39	$39	$39
Ongoing Renewal						
Donors			600	1,080	1,460	3,140
Response rate			80%	80%	80%	80%
Number of gifts			480	864	1,171	2,515
Average gift			$40	$40	$40	$40
Gross revenue			$19,200	$34,560	$46,840	$100,600
Costs			$300	$550	$600	$1,450
Net revenue (expense)			$18,900	$34,010	$46,240	$99,150
Yield per donor			$39	$39	$39	$39
Net revenue (expense)	($8,000)	$15,500	$36,400	$49,510	$61,740	$153,150

Note: Figures are based on five assumptions: (1) 100,000 acquisition packages mailed annually; (2) acquisition response rate of 1 percent; (3) renewal response rate of 60 percent first year, 80 percent thereafter; (4) average gift of acquisition $30, renewal $40; and (5) cost of acquisition at 38¢ each, renewal at 50¢ each.

Exhibit 3.7. Forecast of Revenues from New Fundraising Programs

	Information and Projections	*Forecast*
New-Donor Club		
Number of prospects	_____	
Number of gifts	_____	
Estimated response rate	_____%	
Estimated average gift	$_____	
19__ revenue forecast		$_____
New Corporate Sponsorship Program		
Number of sponsorships	_____	
Number of prospects	_____	
Estimated response rate	_____%	
Estimated number of gifts	_____	
Estimated cost of sponsorship	$_____	
19__ revenue forecast		$_____
Total Forecast of New Programs Revenue for 19__		$_____

annually by the Association for Healthcare Philanthropy (AHP) Foundation in Falls Church, Virginia; *Giving USA,* published annually by the American Association of Fund-Raising Council Trust for Philanthropy in New York; *FRI Survey,* published annually by the Fund Raising Institute in Rockville, Maryland; and *Expenditures in Fund Raising, Alumni Relations, and Other Constituent (Public) Relations* (Council for Advancement and Support of Education and the National Association of College and University Business Officers, 1990). In addition to these sources, the Council for Aid to Education in New York publishes the annual two-volume report *Voluntary Support of Education* and has a wide range of statistical data available in the field of education.

Exhibit 3.8. Net Revenue Forecast for 19__

Revenue Forecast (Gross)

    Contributions unrelated
      to current fundraising
      activities $_____

    Contributions related
      to current fundraising
      activities $_____

    Contributions related to
      new fundraising programs
      to be initiated this year $_____

    Earned income from
      investments $_____

    Other revenues projected $_____

Total Revenue Forecast from
All Sources $_____

Estimated Budget Requirements

    Costs to collect, process,
      and manage gifts unrelated
      to current fundraising
      activities $_____

    Costs to operate the
      established fundraising
      programs (except planned
      giving) $_____

    Costs to establish new
      fundraising programs $_____

    Budget investment in future
      income produced by the
      current year's planned
      giving program $_____

    Other estimated costs $_____

Total estimated costs $_____

Net Revenue Forecast for 19__ $_____

Comparative statistics and other information can also be gathered through the small and informal "peer groups" that have come together around the country. Some of them have developed projects to standardize data collection and reporting procedures for forecasting and evaluation purposes.

As a cross-reference to peer group statistics, Greenfield (1991, p. 46) offers the following reasonable fundraising cost guidelines:

Direct-mail acquisition	$1.00 to $1.25 per dollar raised
Direct-mail renewal	$0.20 per dollar raised
Benefit events	50 percent of gross proceeds
Corporations/foundations	$0.20 per dollar raised
Planned giving	$0.25 per dollar raised
Capital campaigns	$0.05 to $0.10 per dollar raised

Moreover, AHP collects data from its member hospitals each year and publishes a summary report on their giving experience. These annual reports provide valued comparative data by type of health care institutions, bed size and population, size of development office budget, age of development program, size of fundraising staff, and much more. As an illustration, the following table shows the range for return on dollar invested by the age of the programs (AHP Foundation, 1992, p. 4):

Percentiles of Return on Dollar

Age of Program	25%	Median	75%
Under two years	0.8	1.3	3.6
Two to four years	1.2	2.8	4.7
Five to nine years	1.8	3.0	4.1
Ten years or more	2.3	3.3	5.7

The Council of Better Business Bureaus (1982) suggests that overall bottom-line costs not exceed 35 percent of related contributions.

The development of relative fundraising performance standards is an important project for fund professionals and nonprofit institutions.

The abundance of creative activity in this area indicates that these issues are being seriously addressed and that fundraising as a business and public trust is maturing and growing in professionalism.

How to begin

Busy resource development professionals have limited time to implement all of these measurement reports. They can begin with four tasks to arm themselves with the statistical and financial information needed to demonstrate the success of their fundraising programs, to improve performance, to provide the financial information required to meet the public trust, and to justify increased budget investment in new and expanding fundraising programs.

- Determine the information that is needed and design reports that clearly and concisely present that information to the intended audience.

- Develop the internal systems required to obtain accurate financial and statistical information for the reports; obtain relevant external comparative statistics.

- Develop an overall reporting package to present this information in a consistent format on a regular schedule. Regular exposure will help to educate the people who need to know the fundamentals of measuring and evaluating fundraising programs.

- Organize each assessment of future philanthropic potential and new fundraising program financial projections into a one-page, five-year financial projection that includes estimates of revenues, expenses, and net revenues; calculations of rate of return on investment, cost per dollar raised, and dollar production per full-time equivalence; and comparisons with peer group data. The financial projections should be for as many as five years for two reasons. First, the multiyear presentation illustrates that achievement of full program potential is a long-term process. Second, first-year results for some programs will constitute insufficient data to justify the initial required investment.

Conclusion

Moore (1993) predicts that nonprofit institutions and the public will demand greater accountability in health care fundraising. This demand for accountability will require fundraising professionals to demonstrate the productivity and efficiency of their work.

No doubt the forces of scarcity of and competition for financial resources will cause similar demands throughout the nonprofit sector. The 1990s are shaping up as a time of unprecedented challenge for resource development professionals. Effective and appropriate use of the variety of audits and measurements discussed here can help convert challenges into opportunities to improve fundraising performance and to increase net proceeds to our institutions. That is why fundraising professionals are hired in the first place.

References

Association for Healthcare Philanthropy Foundation. *USA Report on Giving, FY 1991*. Falls Church, Va.: Association for Healthcare Philanthropy, 1992.

Costa, N. G. *Measuring Progress and Success in Fundraising: How to Use Comparative Statistics to Prove Effectiveness*. Falls Church, Va.: Association for Healthcare Philanthropy, 1991.

Council for Advancement and Support of Education and National Association of College and University Business Officers. *Expenditures in Fund Raising, Alumni Relations, and Other Constituent (Public) Relations*. Washington, D.C.: Council for Advancement and Support of Education, 1990.

Council of Better Business Bureaus. *Standards for Charitable Solicitations*. Arlington, Va.: Council of Better Business Bureaus, 1982.

Greenfield, J. M. *Fund Raising: Evaluating and Managing the Fund Development Process*. New York: Wiley, 1991.

Greenfield, J. M., and Dreves, J. P. "Fund-Raising Assessment." In T. D. Connors (ed.), *The Nonprofit Management Handbook: Operating Policies and Procedures*. New York: Wiley, 1993.

Moore, M. E. "Effectiveness and Efficiency." In J. M. Greenfield (ed.), *A Healthcare Paradigm: Predicting Change for Healthcare and Philanthropy*. Falls Church, Va.: Association for Healthcare Philanthropy, 1993.

ARTHUR S. COLLIER *is a consultant and senior executive counsel with Ghiorse and Sorrenti, Inc., Woodcliff Lake, New Jersey. An Association for Healthcare Philanthropy (AHP) Fellow, he also is chairman of AHP's university-based programs and director of the annual AHP Institute for Healthcare Philanthropy at the University of Wisconsin, Madison.*

Because of the long delays involved in the cultivation and solicitation of gifts, evaluation of success in fundraising can be difficult. A review of possible evaluation techniques is presented, including suggestions for a new kind of fundraising progress report.

4

Multiyear evaluation of fundraising performance

Wesley E. Lindahl

HOW WELL ARE WE DOING in the fundraising area? How well will we be doing next year? And the year after? Do our fundraising goals represent a reasonable level of possible achievement or are they no better than guesses? These questions are explored year after year by nonprofit organizations that rely on gifts for a sizable portion of their budgets. How well they handle the evaluation process can influence not only the fundraising operation but the entire organization as well.

Most organizations evaluate multiyear fundraising performance by looking at yearly totals and comparing projections (goals) against actual gift levels. Others rely more heavily on comparisons with the prior year's level or national fundraising trends (see Weber, this volume), judging success and setting goals based on these numbers. This basic process is seemingly simple, yet in practice there can be several difficulties for an organization. In this chapter, I describe some of these problems and suggest alternative approaches to answering the question, How are we doing in our fundraising? I begin with the basics on how to project gift levels into the future—the cornerstone to setting reasonable goals.

NEW DIRECTIONS FOR PHILANTHROPIC FUNDRAISING, NO. 3, SPRING 1994 © JOSSEY-BASS PUBLISHERS

Typical projection techniques

Gift data collected over several years become what economists call *time series* data. Methods of projecting time series data into the future are described in any basic text on business or economics statistics (for example, Anderson, Sweeney, and Williams, 1984; Hamburg, 1983; Madsen and Moeschberger, 1983). One of the most simple projections uses the change in level from year 1 to year 2 and assumes that the level for year 3 will change by the same percentage. For example, suppose the gift total for year 1 was $2 million, and the total for year 2 was $2.1 million. The percentage change is 2.1 minus 2.0, divided by 2, and multiplied by 100, or a 5 percent increase. Projecting a 5 percent level of growth for the coming year (multiplying 2.1 by 1.05) provides an estimate of $2.205 million.

Regardless of more fundamental problems to be discussed shortly, this estimate suffers from the fact that only two years are used in the projection, and one or both years may be exceptions for the organization in various ways. A special campaign or an exceptionally large gift may affect only one of these two years. Table 4.1 shows such a scenario. Given the past history of gift levels, the projection for year 8 of $6.95 million is very likely too high, especially if the one year before represented special circumstances.

To solve this problem, projections can be made by incorporating the average of the past several years. Economists have developed a variety of ways to average the past results to project the future. One way to include past data beyond one period is to draw or "fit" a line through all of the data points (years 1 through 7) and use the line to project into the future. This is referred to as a *linear regression projection*. In the above example, a line going most closely through the points would

Table 4.1. Simple Projection Based on Last Year's Growth

			Year				
1	2	3	4	5	6	7	8 (Projected)
300	700	500	400	800	900	2,500	6,950

Note: Figures are in thousands of dollars.

end up at around the $2 million level by year 8 instead of almost $7 million using the simplistic projection. The actual point, if calculated precisely, would be $1,914,286 (−171.429 + 260.7143 × 8). This formula can be determined using any statistics software package, in this case Lotus 1-2-3 (Data/Regression) was used. The problem with this approach is that it assumes a linear trend over the years, when in fact the growth (or decay) may actually follow a nonlinear curve, possibly exponential.

Other techniques are referred to as *smoothing* since they act to smooth out the blips that occur with any series of reported numbers. Smoothing techniques do not assume a linear trend over the entire set of periods. The easiest of these techniques to understand is called *moving averages*. A moving average takes a certain number of periods and adds them together to project the next period. Subsequent periods are determined by dropping the earliest period and adding the most recent into the equation. For example, using data from Table 4.1 and four periods in our moving average, the projection for year 5 would be (year 1 + year 2 + year 3 + year 4) divided by 4 or (300 + 700 + 500 + 400) divided by 4, or 475. Then, to project year 6, year 1 would be dropped and year 5 added. The results would be (700 + 500 + 400 + 800) divided by 4, or 600. Table 4.2 shows the projections versus actual for all possible combinations using the same data set in Table 4.1. The final projection for year 8 of around $1 million is certainly reasonable. However, the projection for year 7 is way off (650 predicted and 2,500 actual). It lagged behind the upward trend, giving too much weight to older data.

Very few economists use moving averages in the simple form described above. More common is the use of exponential smoothing,

Table 4.2. Moving Averages: Actual Over Projected

				Year				
	1	2	3	4	5	6	7	8
Actual	300	700	500	400	800	900	2,500	
Projected					475	600	650	1,150

Note: Figures are in thousands of dollars.

where all past data are used in the calculation of the next period. In addition, variable weights can be assigned to the more recent years over the older years. In comparison, simple moving averages always lend equal weights to each year. The formula for exponential smoothing is as follows:

$$F_{t+1} = wY_t + (1-w)F_t$$

where F_{t+1} is the forecast for the next period, Y_t is the actual value for the current period, F_t is the projection for the current period, w is a constant between 0 and 1 that shows how much weight to give to the most recent year, and $(1-w)$ is the resulting constant that shows how much weight to give to the older years.

To come up with an estimate for the coming year (F_{t+1}), we need only provide the current value (Y_t) and the current projected value (F_t). This makes the projection system easy to use. In 1990, Northwestern University used a slight variation on exponential smoothing (double exponential smoothing) to provide the estimates for 1991 through 1994 presented in Table 4.3. The two columns in Table 4.3 show the

Table 4.3. Northwestern University 1990 Projections Using Double Exponential Smoothing

Year	Actual	Projected w = .3	Projected w = .7
1983	34.2		
1984	36.1		
1985	46.5		
1986	49.3		
1987	57.3		
1988	65.9		
1989	68.7		
1990	68.0		
1991	70.9[a]	71.4	68.9
1992	102.6[a]	74.4	69.1
1993		77.5	69.5
1994		80.5	69.8

Note: Figures are in millions of dollars.

[a] Value is included to show how 1990 four-year projections compare to actual figures.

difference when using a constant w of .3 versus .7. The lower number puts less weight on the recent years. In highly volatile time series, a lower number (w) will project more accurately (Anderson, Sweeney, and Williams, 1984, p. 521).

Development effort

One of the problems in using past projections is the failure to consider the effort exerted by the development operation over the years—the effort levels both before and after the goal setting process. The 1992 actual giving level for Northwestern University, presented in Table 4.3, could be partially anticipated if the level of development activity in the past were taken into account. Perhaps no one could predict the extent of the rise in gift dollars, but certainly the flat prediction of the $w = .7$ projection (Table 4.3) would be rejected outright as unrealistic. Use of past development effort to help project future giving is informative even if the total levels of past development effort or activity are relatively constant. In these cases, there might be variations in the amount of activity of the various programs within the fundraising operation. Any long-range evaluation process must view the development results as driven in part by the amount of projected effort in the operation.

Measurement of development effort is not always straightforward. The total fundraising budget level provides a start. Activities such as telephone calls, personal visits, letters, and direct-mail appeals can also be tracked and used as measures of activity. Organizations such as the Council for Advancement and Support of Education (CASE) and the National Association of College and University Business Officers (NACUBO) have provided guidelines for reporting costs (CASE and NACUBO, 1990), which can be substituted for effort in most cases.

Whatever approach is used to track development effort, is there any empirical evidence of a quantifiable link between effort and results? Research through the past twenty years has indeed shown a direct relationship between effort and results in nonprofit fundraising (J. Leslie, 1969, 1979; Pickett, 1977, 1982; L. Leslie and Ramey, 1985; Loessin,

Duronio, and Borton, 1987). For example, Loessin, Duronio, and Borton (1987) found that for all institutional types in higher education,
total voluntary support correlated highly (over .70) with expenditures
for fundraising. Precise estimation of the relationship for a particular
program is not easy, but the theory suggests that the task is worthwhile.

There are several possible models that could be used to project gift
levels in view of development effort. Paton (1986) and Steinberg
(1985) have discussed what such a relationship might look like. Both
show a model that begins with some level of gifts coming in without
much effort. With increasing effort, the level of gifts stays stable due to
the high cost of setting up a particular fundraising program. After a
certain threshold is reached, the curve moves up sharply, reflecting the
efficiency of the program. However, beyond a certain point, the capacity and interest of the market reach maximum saturation and the
curve levels out. Any increase in funding now will produce little if any
growth in gift revenue. Figure 4.1 illustrates the general shape of such
a curve based on the hypothetical data set from Tables 4.1 and 4.2.
Using this curve visually to project the gift level for year 8, and assum-

Figure 4.1. General Model Relating Development Effort and Gifts

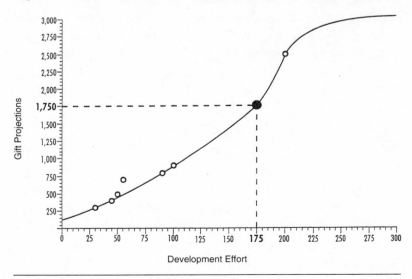

Note: Figures are in thousands of dollars.

ing a development effort level of $175,000, we can anticipate a gift level of around $1.75 million. Table 4.4 shows the corresponding effort and gift level for years 1–8 (8 is projected).

Besides a visual approach to setting up a curve to relate effort and gifts, there are more sophisticated methods as well. One approach uses the general form of a standard sales force response curve. The specific version used at Northwestern is the same form as used to project sales based on changes in the level of the sales force in an industrial setting (Sinha and Zoltners, 1986; Zoltners and Sinha, 1980). The adapted mathematical model (configured specifically for fundraising) states that for each category, this year's gift level is a combination of three values: no-effort gifts, past-effort gifts, and current-effort gifts (Lindahl, 1992a, p. 67).

At Northwestern, we have developed specific models for our various fundraising programs and then combined them into an overall formula. The process of estimating the coefficients in the models involves the combination of historical analysis and the collective judgments (estimates) of the development staff.

These models can be useful beyond the process of projecting future gift levels. Because of the link between effort and gifts, they can be used in the process of resource allocation, one of the central economic issues for fundraising (see Steinberg, this volume). Resource allocation is a major part of the strategic planning process, and a nonprofit organization can determine the best action plan for the coming time period by optimizing these equations (Lindahl, 1992a), a process based on the concept of marginal returns (see Steinberg, this volume).

Of course, any model is only an estimate and is only as good as the

Table 4.4. Effort-Based Projections

				Year				
	1	2	3	4	5	6	7	8
Effort	30	55	50	45	90	100	200	175
Gifts	300	700	500	400	800	900	2,500	
Projections								1,750

Note: Figures are in thousands of dollars.

information available at the time. Certainly one source of inaccuracy could stem from differences in the level of quality in the development effort. Especially in a small fundraising office (one or two staff members), the success of the operation often hinges on how well the members implement the development effort, rather than just the sheer dollars allocated to the office. In a larger department, with ten to thirty officers, the quality of the development effort will vary around some average, and the allocated dollars will become more representative of actual effort levels. Quality can be improved through training and practice. The resources dedicated to the development effort might be spent on conferences or other training to improve the activities of the staff. Models could be developed that account for this factor. Because Northwestern has over thirty development officers, this factor was not incorporated into the model.

Time delays in fundraising

The effort-driven model described above is built on the idea that a certain amount of the success in fundraising is determined not only by this year's effort level but also by the effort put forth over the past years. Decreasing weight is given to the earlier years. This factor is very important to consider in the gift-raising process, because the time delay between when a prospect is cultivated and solicited and when the gift is eventually received can be quite extensive.

In Lindahl (1990, 1992b), I investigated time delays for fundraising in two different settings. In Lindahl (1990), the lengths of time from the point of solicitation to when the gift arrived for a selected sample of prospects were observed. The analysis of the delay factors involved in the solicitation streams revealed a great difference among the various categories (or fundraising programs) in the study. Most categories had delays within the time frame of the study (six years). Some of the categories had delays that appeared to go outside the bounds of the study.

For example, direct-mail and phon-a-thon responses represented less than a year's delay between the solicitation and the gift. Major gifts from all sources had delays of four and five years from major solicitation activity until the final payment on a multiyear pledge. Bequests and irrevocable trusts could not be analyzed properly within a six-year period. A minimum of fifteen years of data is probably required to determine the appropriate delay factors involved for deferred gifts. Sharpe's (1991) analysis of bequests given during the depression of the 1930s further supports this conclusion. He reported that the mix of bequests and outright gifts was heavily skewed toward bequests during this time period. I conclude that these bequests, received during the depression, were in the "pipeline," having been set up many years before. The bequests held the overall gift levels steady (or slightly down), even as outright giving, with a shorter time delay, dropped precipitously. The results support the idea that development is a very long-term process.

In Lindahl (1992b), I looked at all individual donors of gifts over $50,000 in the five years 1986–1990 at Northwestern University. Donors were put into categories based on their past giving behavior, alumni status, and type of gift. Fifty-five percent of the gifts came from the four most popular categories (121 out of 233 gifts). The following brief description of the donors in each of these four categories reveals the extent and overall time involved in successful cultivation processes. Unsuccessful cultivation could potentially be even longer, depending on the tenacity of the development staff (and the unwillingness of the prospect!).

Alumni giving outright gifts ($50,000 or more) after giving over $1,000 in the past. The great majority of these repeat donors had extensive contact over many decades both with the development staff directly and via other university activities (John Evans Club, the highest-level gift club; associates; visiting committees; trustees; awards; events; and so on). Those with little or no contact often had a second party in the transaction (relative, family foundation, and so on).

Nonalumni giving outright gifts ($50,000 or more) after giving over $1,000 in the past. Most of these donors were involved as trustees or associates and had extensive contact with the university and the development office (between ten and fifty-nine years). Other donors had less long-term contact and were past patients of medical school staff doctors, parents, or community philanthropists. Contact increased after the first gift.

Alumni giving an irrevocable trust gift ($50,000 or more) after giving an irrevocable trust gift (any size) in the past. Since these donors had already set up at least one irrevocable trust, they were contacted and visited by staff of the Planned and Major Gift (PMG) Office on a regular basis over a period of five to ten or more years, including contact related to the earlier gifts. Some donors had long involvement in campus activities beyond the PMG contact.

Alumni giving an irrevocable trust gift ($50,000 or more) after giving some outright gift under $1,000 in the past. Almost all donors self-identified via responses to a Dealing-in-Futures (DIF) planned giving mailer. Typical time from DIF response to gift was five to ten years (although for two donors the time frame was over twenty years, and for one donor, one year). Almost all contact was moderate, consisting mainly of personal visits by PMG staff.

Since most of a nonprofit organization's gift dollars come from a very small number of high-level contributors, the results from the four categories of $50,000-or-more donors represent a large part of the reported gift totals. Time delays of five to ten years between cultivation and results could certainly cause difficulty when projecting future fundraising results. The problem is not limited to the major-gift program. Even with direct-mail and phon-a-thon solicitations, where the lengths of time are usually much shorter, the work done in years past can play a role in bringing in today's gifts. Any model intended to project gift levels accurately needs to incorporate this delay or carryover effect.

Organizational goals

Because of the long time frame involved in fundraising, the evaluation process should incorporate ways to track the current year's extent and quality of the contacts with prospects. At Northwestern, the development office maintains a record of all calls made to prospects. The

Planned and Major Gift Office aggregates its results annually, showing how many prospects were contacted and the type of contacts that were made (telephone call versus personal visit). The phon-a-thon program keeps track of the number of calls attempted and made each year, and the direct-mail program audits the number of pieces sent under each solicitation. Goals can be set in these areas as well. Murray (1987) has discussed possible additional areas where goals can be set. Evaluation of progress each year would consider how closely the nonmonetary goals were set.

Besides the difficulty with time delays, there are other reasons why use of the typical reporting format—grand total gifts given in the year—can distort the task of evaluation. Some gifts, because of restrictions on spending, are less valuable to the organization than are unrestricted gifts. Some restricted gifts can be "funged" or transferred to other areas by budgeting differently. An endowed gift, with restrictions on spending the principal, affects an organization differently from a gift for operations. There is higher risk associated with the former because of the uncertainty of the discount rates in calculating the income from the endowment over the years. The value of gifts beyond the cash value should be considered in determining if the development office is meeting its goals.

Ultimately, the organization's overall goals, for example, to build a new science education building or feed fifteen thousand hungry people each year, must be considered in any evaluation of development progress. The cash and activity numbers are usually easier to gather, especially in a large nonprofit organization, but monitoring of the final organizational goals is what really matters. Evaluation of success in meeting these overall goals is often qualitative, but it usually can be stated in a way that allows for verification of completion.

New report

Central to the task of evaluating fundraising success is the creation of an enhanced development report based on the principles outlined in this chapter. While the typical gift-reporting practices, as recommended by organizations such as the Council for Aid to Education (CFAE), CASE, NACUBO, and the Financial Accounting Standards Board (FASB), provide an excellent view of the results of fundraising across the entire organization and back into time, they do not allow the organization to monitor the success of the development staff in the current year of operation (see Collier, this volume). Changes are under way in these standards that parallel some of the ideas presented here, for example, with pledge reporting (see Larkin, this volume). However, most of these accounting changes are geared toward better reporting of the financial condition of the organization rather than better reporting of the success of the fundraising operation.

There is a report structure that provides a better evaluation tool for fundraising. Because of the problems with the delay factor in fundraising, pledges should be considered, whereas pledge payments should be eliminated from the report. The pledges should be adjusted to reflect the length of time over which they will be paid, assuming a certain cost of money over the coming years. Think of having to borrow the balance on the pledge throughout the pledge period at some rate. The interest charged during this time must be paid from the pledge payments. Most nonprofit organizations do not borrow against pledges. However, they still need to consider the lost opportunity costs in these cases.

The following three examples show how this technique works. A $40,000 pledge paid out over four years of $10,000 payments is only worth $31,698.65 (assuming 10 percent cost of capital), or only 79 percent of the pledge amount. A $200,000 pledge paid by two $100,000 annual payments is worth $180,801.80 (with an 8 percent cost of capital), or only 90 percent of the pledge amount. If the length of the pledge period is unknown, the analyst can assume a typical three-year payout with a 10 percent cost of money and use 80 percent of the pledge amount as a rough estimate for the current value of the pledge. Most spreadsheet programs provide automatic functions to calculate present values. For example, in Lotus 1-2-3 the function is @NPV(interest,range).

Although not completely necessary, an adjustment could even be made to reduce the pledges by an expected rate of default, if that is a significant occurrence for an organization (see Larkin, this volume). To illustrate this adjustment with the second example from the above discussion, a $200,000 pledge might first be reduced to $180,801.80. Then, because only 70 percent of all pledges are typically ever fulfilled at the organization, the $180,801.80 is reduced to 70 percent, or $126,561.26.

The second change to the standard method of recording gifts involves bequests. These gifts cause problems because of the very long delay between when the gift is solicited and when it finally comes to the institution at the donor's death. Also, because bequests are revocable, the organization should consider the long-term costs of maintaining the relationship over the life of the donor. For example, a bequest expectancy might be set up to fund a special department of classics within the College of Arts and Sciences. In order for the donor relationship to be maintained over the years, the university is obligated to keep the College of Arts and Sciences prepared to offer such a program, for example, to maintain at least one instructor in the classics, until the donor dies.

Therefore, bequests should be handled similarly to pledges. A portion of bequest expectancies should be counted at the time when the bequest is set up and reported to the institution. The amount counted can be determined by actuarial tables and by considering the necessary long-term obligations to ensure that the bequest is not revoked before the donor dies. If one assumes a twenty-year period of delay and a 10 percent cost of money, 30 percent can be used as a base estimate for those cases where the exact age of the donor is unknown. If the amount is unknown, the median bequest received amount for the current year can be used. When bequests actually come in, they should be eliminated from the current-year gifts reported. Bequests that come in without a prior bequest expectancy on file should not be counted either, since little direct development effort was probably expended to bring in the particular gift. A case-by-case process could be used since so few bequest transactions are recorded each year by an organization.

Counting of bequests using this approach is in contrast to the more conservative stance of the FASB standards (see Larkin, this volume). Development officers who spend time working with prospects to set up bequests need a way to record success in this area this year instead of twenty years from now, hence the more liberal methodology.

Removal of low-development-effort gifts is the third suggested change. Especially in large education institutions, gifts can arrive and be counted in the development office without any prior action or knowledge of the development staff. Research grants that are solicited directly by the principal investigator are prime examples. These transactions should be eliminated from the report, whenever possible. They certainly reflect the organization's success in research, but they are in the way when development progress is measured.

The fourth change involves irrevocable trusts (see Larkin, this volume). Normally, these gifts are counted at the total market value at the time when the trust is set up. This number should be adjusted to reflect the gift's true value to the institution. This can be a difficult task, since the gift may set up an annuity that will pay an income stream to more than one person over each of their lifetimes. At Northwestern, we recently gained control of the principal of an annuity that was set up over forty years ago. Correct estimation of the true cash value in the 1940s would have been nearly impossible. In those cases where it is difficult to determine a value, a certain percentage of total market value might be agreed to in advance by all parties involved. This approach should be used only in difficult cases.

Once the donor or other specified individual dies, the dollars that created the annuity trust are made available to the nonprofit organization (see Larkin, this volume). These funds must not be double-counted as gifts when they are finally accessible to the organization. If the nonprofit organization is the trustee of the trust, this is usually not a problem since the funds are recorded in the accounting ledgers when the gift is given originally (Larkin, this volume). When the organization is not the trustee, but only the beneficiary, a bank is usually the trustee. In this case, the development office may have originally counted the gift when notified of the trust's existence, but the accounting department may not have recorded the transaction. When the principal is released to the nonprofit organization, the accounting department will count the money, but the development office should not count the money a second time (even if the value has increased over the years).

After these four adjustments to pledges, bequests, low-development-effort gifts, and irrevocable trusts are made, totals by category going back several years are determined. Most institutions have computer systems that can be programmed to produce the proper results. At Northwestern, we began generating these numbers on a trial basis in 1989. Initially, we had difficulty in completely identifying low-development-effort gifts, hence only the most obvious gifts (from private agencies and associations) were removed for this analysis. Table 4.5 shows how the adjusted numbers reveal a different pattern of success as compared to the standard CFAE methodology.

In Table 4.5, the success registered in the adjusted total more closely relates to development effort in the respective year. For example, in 1990, the $89.3 million adjusted level included over $55 million in pledges (using current valuation) that will be paid off in the years to come. The $102.6 million CFAE total in 1992 reflects the payments from the record pledge levels of 1989 and 1990, $4.3 million in gifts with low development effort, and a very large bequest ($12 million). This bequest was removed from the adjusted numbers because it was reported to Northwestern many years ago. Although the adjusted numbers appear much more volatile, they actually reflect what often happens in a typical fundraising setting and in the national economy (notice the downturn in 1991).

Table 4.5. Modified Report of Development Progress: Northwestern University

Year	CFAE Total	Adjusted Total
1989	68.7	80.1
1990	68.0	89.3
1991	70.9	40.2
1992	102.6	60.8

Note: Figures are in millions of dollars; CFAE = Council for Aid to Education.

Finally, the organization can develop a new combined internal progress report. The first section of the report includes the adjusted monetary results as previously described. The figures, subdivided by fundraising program, are compared to goals (set using effort-based models). The second section reports the development activity levels (number of calls, letters sent, and so on), compared once again to goal levels. The third section reviews the achievements of the organization in those areas affected by donations. How well did the development operation assist the organization in achieving the overriding goals? Evaluations based on such reporting and goal setting will help the nonprofit organization reach goals with the highest degree of effectiveness and efficiency possible.

References

Anderson, D. R., Sweeney, D. J., and Williams, T. A. *Statistics for Business and Economics.* Saint Paul, Minn.: West, 1984.

Council for Advancement and Support of Education (CASE) and National Association of College and University Business Officers (NACUBO). *Expenditures in Fund Raising, Alumni Relations, and Other Constituent (Public) Relations.* Washington, D.C.: Council for Advancement and Support of Education, 1990.

Hamburg, M. *Statistical Analysis for Decision Making.* Orlando, Fla.: Harcourt Brace Jovanovich, 1983.

Leslie, J. W. *Focus on Understanding and Support: A Study in College Management.* Washington, D.C.: American College Public Relations Association, 1969.

Leslie, J. W. "Variations in Fund-Raising Potential Among Colleges and Universities." In W. Heeman (ed.), *Analyzing the Cost-Effectiveness of Fund Raising.* New Directions for Institutional Advancement, no. 3. San Francisco: Jossey-Bass, 1979.

Leslie, L. L., and Ramey, G. "When Donors Give: How Giving Changes in Good and Bad Times." *CASE Currents,* 1985, *11* (9), 25–26.

Lindahl, W. E. "Resource Allocation in University Fund Raising." Unpublished doctoral dissertation, School of Education and Social Policy, Northwestern University, 1990.

Lindahl, W. E. *Strategic Planning for Fund Raising: How to Bring in More Money Using Strategic Resource Allocation.* San Francisco: Jossey-Bass, 1992a.

Lindahl, W. E. "Success in Major Gift Fund Raising." Unpublished manuscript, Northwestern University, 1992b.

Loessin, B. A., Duronio, M. A., and Borton, G. L. "Identifying Peer Institutions for Comparative Evaluation of Fund Raising Effectiveness." Paper presented at the Association of Institutional Research Forum, Kansas City, Mo., May 1987.

Madsen, R. W., and Moeschberger, M. L. *Introductory Statistics for Business and Economics.* Englewood Cliffs, N.J.: Prentice Hall, 1983.

Murray, D. *The Guaranteed Fund-Raising System: A Systems Approach to Planning and Controlling Fund Raising.* Poughkeepsie, N.Y.: American Institute of Management, 1987.

Paton, G. J. "Microeconomic Perspectives Applied to Developmental Planning and Management." In J. A. Dunn (ed.), *Enhancing the Management of Fund Raising.* New Directions for Institutional Research, no. 51. San Francisco: Jossey-Bass, 1986.

Pickett, W. L. "An Assessment of the Effectiveness of Fund Raising Policies of Private Undergraduate Colleges." Unpublished doctoral dissertation, Department of Higher Education, University of Denver, 1977.

Pickett, W. L. "What Determines Fund Raising Effectiveness?" *CASE Currents,* 1982, 8 (1), 22–25.

Sharpe, R. F. *Philanthropy in Uncertain Times.* Unpublished manuscript, Robert F. Sharpe and Company, 1991.

Sinha, P., and Zoltners, A. *Addressing the Issues of Sales Force Size and Structure.* Evanston, Ill.: ZS Associates, 1986.

Steinberg, R. "Optimal Fundraising by Nonprofit Firms." In *Giving and Volunteering: New Frontiers of Knowledge.* 1985 Spring Research Forum Working Papers. New York: INDEPENDENT SECTOR and United Way Institute, 1985.

Zoltners, A., and Sinha, P. "Integer Programming Models for Sales Resource Allocation." *Management Science,* 1980, *26,* 242–260.

WESLEY E. LINDAHL *is director of development and alumni information services at Northwestern University, Evanston, Illinois, and is a researcher on the topic of fundraising economics and philanthropy.*

Major donors are concerned about administrative costs in fundraising, but their perceptions are based on their relationships to professional staff or other major givers. This chapter explores the connection between perceptions and giving patterns.

5

Effects of administrative cost perceptions in major-gift decisions

Gary A. Tobin

FUNDRAISING INSTITUTIONS are faced with growing and increasingly complex challenges. New fundraising techniques are required, and established, successful fundraising techniques must be expanded. Both require a better understanding of major donors.

Major donors and fundraising efforts

This chapter examines the philanthropic behavior and attitudes of major donors to Jewish philanthropies, and the effects of perceptions of fundraising costs on their giving. With rare exception, fundraising efforts in the Jewish community depend on the major gifts that comprise a high percentage of the total funds that are raised. Without the few but vital major gifts, any fundraising effort is likely to fall short of its goal. But the recruitment and solicitation of major donors takes place in an increasingly complex fundraising environment. Individuals with the potential for large contributions are targeted by a multi-

NEW DIRECTIONS FOR PHILANTHROPIC FUNDRAISING, NO. 3, SPRING 1994 © JOSSEY-BASS PUBLISHERS

tude of organizations, agencies, institutions, and causes, both in the Jewish and non-Jewish communities. The competition for major gifts is more intense than ever before. Jewish donors are solicited constantly. While there has been an increase in information about the attitudes and behaviors of Jews in terms of giving patterns, volunteerism, and participation in the fundraising world, little systematic attention has been given to the attitudes and behaviors of major donors in the Jewish community. Given that they play such a critical role in the overall health of the fundraising system, information about them is essential. Perceptions of fundraising costs are an important area of inquiry in understanding the overall patterns of major-donor giving.

In this chapter, I summarize the findings of a study of major Jewish philanthropists throughout the United States. I conducted in-depth personal interviews and focus groups in cities throughout the United States, including Boston, San Francisco, communities in Southern Florida, and elsewhere. Over one hundred personal interviews were conducted with individuals who contribute at least $10,000 per year to philanthropies, and focus groups were assembled to explore the attitudes of similar givers. The data collected illuminate the motivations for giving, how the donors select philanthropies to which to contribute, and the role of attitudes about fundraising costs.

Factors affecting the decision to give

Donors give primarily because it makes them feel fulfilled, based on a sense of moral, ethical, or religious obligation. Status, reward, and peer group influence serve as reinforcing factors, but usually in a context where the donor already feels a personal sense of moral accomplishment.

This commitment as a moral obligation, a general desire to support the community, to help others, to support the needy, and other such expressions are the key motivators for contributions to Jewish philanthropies. Major gifts are tied to the perception that something good is accomplished through the contribution. While recognition, face-to-face solicitations, and other techniques may be utilized to build on a general commitment or to help develop these feelings in individuals, they cannot substitute for these more compelling moral motivations. Technique cannot substitute for substance. The extent to which perceptions of fundraising costs do or do not reinforce this primary sense of mission is a key factor in the decision to give. The major donors sampled in my research were unwilling to say what proportions of their incomes—2 percent, 5 percent, 10 percent, or more—should be allocated for philanthropies. They were unwilling to set standards but said that they give what they can afford. Their philanthropy is part of an ad hoc budgetary process, and therefore their feelings about fundraising costs are equally unclear.

Nearly all of the major donors said that they could give much more to philanthropies if they believed strongly enough in the purpose. But major donors cannot always be convinced that their funds will make a difference. Donors wish to be shown, for example, the direct connection between their gifts and a particular program. They all want to be sure that their money will be well spent. But demonstration of programmatic effectiveness is very difficult, and image and other vague factors influence overall perceptions.

Involvement as a major donor is an alternate track to an individual's personal experience with a particular cause. While personal interests may be the best vehicle for an immediate and deep commitment to the particular purpose of an organization, individuals may develop an equally deep commitment by becoming involved with the organization as volunteers. Such involvement may originate in a business or social contact, a sense of civic obligation, or a perfunctory agreement to participate that evolves over time into a major role. The major donors in my study indicated that they were involved in at least one philanthropy of which they had little or no knowledge at the outset, but they became deeply committed because of their increased participation within the organizational structure. Requests to participate on boards or committees, of course, are as frequent as requests for donations. Therefore, "noise level" is also problematic in efforts to recruit major donors to be board or committee members. They will respond, however, to a limited number of requests for causes that can be demonstrated to be important and worthwhile. Perceptions of fundraising costs are framed within this context, either from afar with little personal evaluation or after the donor becomes involved and forms impressions from within the organization.

Task orientation

Many major donors would rather be involved in a specific project than serve on a board or committee. The more limited and targeted the task, the more likely it is that the donor will agree to participate. Since they are as interested in guarding their time as they are their financial resources, requests for participation are screened as carefully as requests for donations. Therefore, a business contact, a social peer, or someone with a personal tie to the individual is much more likely to have success in eliciting participation than is a person who is unknown to the donor.

Mailbox glut

Major donors do not read most of the written materials mailed to them from philanthropic organizations. They are bombarded not only by requests for money and time but also by direct mail, important messages, and other written materials that describe various philanthropic causes. One donor mused, "How much mail should I be getting? Maybe about 30 percent of it. It is not targeted. It is pretty general. I get general pieces that are 'Dear Contributor,' or something like that, and I am not going to go forward with the reading of the letter" (Tobin, 1990c).

Given the constraints on their time, it is almost impossible for major donors to read even a small proportion of the vast amounts of written materials that are sent to them. They are most likely to read one-page bulletins that are written in bullet language; that is, where major points are made, crisply presented, and easy to digest. They are also more likely to read and absorb materials that are handed to them, that are well prepared, visually pleasant, and easy to read, and that are discussed in a personal meeting. One interviewee, upon examining a direct-mail piece, stated, "If this is something that is mailed out to every person in the community, it is way overstated. It is too complex. Someone going through mounds and mounds of mail will not want to read all of this" (Tobin, 1990a). Another donor had this to say about a piece of direct mail that he was examining: "It's written in the wrong mode. Stop asking questions, because people will get the impression that you have no idea what you're talking about. If you make it declarative, make it affirmative, say something and don't ask questions, then you've got something that focuses thought" (Tobin, 1992a).

Nearly all materials that come through the mail, including minutes of board meetings or executive summaries, even of organizations in which the donors are involved, go mostly unread. The written word, especially if it is distributed through the mail, as a means of increasing a donor's knowledge and involvement often has minimal positive influence. The amount of mail and the kind of mail, however, influence perceptions of the agency: It is well organized, efficient, and managing its money well?

Personal touch

Personal contact with the organization is essential for continued interest and involvement of major donors, and through this contact most perceptions of overhead are formed. Many donors feel that they only hear from the organization when it solicits them, and because they do not read the written information sent through the mail, they do not feel that they have enough knowledge about or positive personal contact with the organization. Therefore, their perceptions of fundraising costs are generally vague. One-on-one meetings with the organization's executive director or lay officers are an important form of personal contact. Individual breakfast meetings, luncheons, or other informal information-sharing sessions keep the donor well informed and connected to the organization. Telephone calls from the organization's executive director or another lay person for the purpose of informing the donor about events or activities of the organization serve a far greater purpose than can be achieved through the mail. The more personal contact the donor has with someone from the organization, the more likely he or she is to continue to make a major contribution or to increase the giving level and feel comfortable with the organization.

Personal contact also includes greater personal interaction with the recipients or beneficiaries of the donor's gift. Structured visits to a hospital, a museum, a university, or whatever organization is being funded

are essential. However, tours of buildings and meetings with administrators have less impact than close-up views of the programs that are
funded, as well as meetings with the clients and more "human" expe-
riences. Numbers and abstract descriptions need to be personalized as
much as possible so that the donor feels more engaged and can see the
results of the funded programs. As one interviewee stated, "I always
say that periodically it is a very good thing to spend a few hours at
Children's Hospital and see what the real world is all about. . . . You
get a very real feeling of the world, for what things are, and being
thankful that you don't need these facilities" (Tobin, 1990b).

Similarly, donors need continual positive feedback about their gifts.
They need to be shown in detail, and frequently, how their monies are
being spent, what good is being accomplished through their gifts, the
positive progress that is being made, and how these results could not
be achieved without their participation. One donor called for more
personal contact: "There is nothing like a face-to-face meeting. I don't
think that it would take very long to see all of the major donors, even
one-on-one, just to explain next year's campaign, just to say this is
where we are and this is what the problems will be if we don't get there,
this is what your money is going to go to, this is why we need it"
(Tobin, 1990d).

Thank-you letters or general brochures cannot substitute for the
one-on-one contact that is achieved through the kind of informal and
personalized meetings described above. These meetings should not be
held for the purpose of solicitation but rather to make donors feel good
about the monies that they have donated, and to provide the positive
feedback necessary throughout the year so that the donors stay engaged with the organization. Without positive feedback, donors are
likely to feel less committed to an organization and, therefore, unsure
about its level of efficiency and good management.

Role of the solicitor

Donors are very aware of what they consider an excellent, mediocre,
or poor solicitation. A positive or negative impression about a solicitor creates an overall impression of the organization. Many donors do

not distinguish between the people who solicit them and the organization as a whole. Since the solicitors represent the organization, the way in which they present themselves, the character of the solicitation, and other attributes of the individuals are ascribed to the organization. These factors, of course, can have long-term implications. One negative solicitation may sustain a poor image of that organization for many years. Once a negative solicitation has taken place, it is increasingly difficult to positively solicit a major donor. It is through the solicitor that images of fundraising costs are often formed.

Three primary attributes describe a positive and best solicitor: knowledgeable, committed, and passionate. Knowledgeable includes information about how much of a gift goes to overhead. This information is important because major donors are also very concerned about the efficiency of the organization. The proportion of dollars that is actually expended for the purposes for which money is donated plays a role in the amount of the gift that a major donor considers giving. In the words of one interviewee: "[There is] concern about the administrative costs that are involved. Twenty percent of your giving is going to administrative costs. You can give directly to a cause and eliminate those administrative costs. That is a way to generate 20 percent more giving. I know the expense is there. I think a lot of it can be eliminated."

The higher the percentage given for direct program support, the more likely major donors are to positively consider the organization. Some organizations are at a disadvantage because of their relatively high administrative costs. Other organizations that actually have high levels of efficiency do not always promote this aspect of their administrative structures as well as they might.

Perceptions of fundraising costs

Among the important factors in the decision to give and how much to give are the perceived purpose of the organization, the nature of the solicitation, the specific cause that appeals to the donor, peer influence, the donor's own assessment of his or her ability to give (how much he or she can afford), tax benefits, social status, and the desire to do good. Donors do not give because an organization is deemed efficient or inefficient. This is a factor of selection of a philanthropy and level of commitment to it, but not a basic motivator per se.

On balance, most major donors do not think very much about fundraising costs as such. The overall efficiency of an organization is judged by many factors, including the perceived quality of the services that are provided, their impressions of the professional staff, the level of interest in the cause. Donors may be apprehensive about the use of their donation, but they do not spend much time investigating actual overhead. In terms of ease of examination for donors, there are also differences in fundraising costs between organizations that have fundraising as their primary purpose and organizations that have a fundraising component. Universities, hospitals, and cultural arts institutions, for example, may have significant development departments that are generally unknown or unnoticed (certainly not assessed) by many major donors. University presidents, department heads, and other non–fundraising professionals may devote a considerable part of their time to fundraising but are not considered part of the administrative budget, whereas professionals in fundraising are always considered part of the fundraising costs. On the other hand, umbrella organizations such as the United Jewish Appeal and the United Way, which are seen as exclusively fundraising, are easier to examine: What percentages of funds raised are distributed for their designated purposes.

Donor attitudes about the costs of fundraising are characterized by conflicting feelings and contradictions. Most attitudes are molded by general impressions, images, and random assessments of philanthropies in general and of particular organizations as well. The perceptions of fundraising costs are part of a large bundle of motivators and inhibitors to giving, how much is given, and which causes. But the influences are subtle and indirect.

The donor's difficulty in assessing fundraising costs is easily understood: It is difficult for the most sophisticated observer to comprehend comparative fundraising costs. As noted by Greene (1992, p. 26), "Experts caution that it is often difficult to determine a charity's efficiency without knowing more about its age, programs, management, and accounting methods. What's more, variations in non-profits' overhead and fundraising costs sometimes owe as much to the difference in their program areas as to the effectiveness of their management."

While some donors in my study were vague and negative about fund-raising costs, others were just as vague but positive. When asked if a particular organization was efficient, a donor of $50,000 said, "I think so. You can always find more efficient, but I think so. I am not saying that they are doing a perfect job, but we can always try and change it too." These views were expressed by a person who had generally positive views of the organization's mission, professionals, and volunteers.

Donors tend to evaluate efficiency and overhead, and react positively or negatively to fundraising costs, based on how they feel in general about an organization. Many feel that if an organization projects a positive image, it is probably well run. Many donors are not willing to become involved to the point where they know enough to properly evaluate the organization. For example, one interviewee in my study said,

I have a philosophy. I accept that [Jewish organization] is doing good things. I've crossed that bridge. Unless I am prepared to really get involved deeply, I don't think that I am going to be in a better position to say should I give them a 95 percent grade or a 90 percent grade or 80 percent grade. I have accepted that their grade is up there and, therefore, I'm not sure that it really improves the quality of my decision making about where to allocate my resources unless I am really prepared to look at it pretty deeply, and I am not. I am trusting the people that I have respect for. I know a lot of them, so that is the way that I feel about it. And, therefore, to listen to what they are doing in more detail for an hour or two hours, I'm not sure really benefits anybody [Tobin, 1992b].

Major donors expect fundraising organizations to reinforce the culture of giving by providing positive feedback, keeping the donor informed, and helping the donor feel good about giving. At the same time, donors expect the organization to be more businesslike. One donor noted that people will complain that an organization does not thank them enough and then complain about a dinner to celebrate the closing of a campaign: "Even when you go to a dinner, I understand that they can't make it totally elaborate because then people will go in and think, 'Well, look where my money is going. It's going for the flowers. It's going for the food. It's not going where it should go.' People are like that. It's almost as if, I think, that if they would spend more money on their flowers and on their food and on the ambiance, people would think of it more as a party and enjoy being there. I don't know if people do look around. I've heard that that's what people would think, and so they tend to streamline what they do. But I think people like to see the ambiance and the prettiness and the fun and the party spirit as well" (Tobin, 1989b).

The task of disseminating information about fundraising costs is itself a risky undertaking. Major donors do not have some commonly understood standard of efficiency, low or high overhead, frugality or waste. A 15 percent overhead figure may seem wonderfully efficient to one donor and extremely wasteful to another. Selective comparisons to other organizations may help or hinder, depending on the image of the organization in the first place. The cost of fundraising can only be assessed as a positive or a negative in the context of many other factors. Information about fundraising costs as a sole consideration is not likely to reassure most major donors.

Some donors take an active interest in overhead costs during the solicitation process. They may ask questions about how much of their gifts will support the project. These queries tend to occur more frequently with specific projects as opposed to annual giving. The role of the solicitor is most important in the context of addressing the issue of overhead: "If I give money, I want to make sure where the money goes—at least 90 percent to what I am intending it for. When I built the gymnasium, I said, 'what does it cost?' I have built a few buildings in my time and I know what it costs. I don't believe that money should be made on charity. In my business, yes; but on charity, no" (Tobin, 1992b).

The more complex an organization, the more likely a donor is to perceive that the organization has unnecessary overhead, administrative costs, and bureaucratic waste. In some ways, the organizational complexity necessary for successful fundraising carries with it a stigma of excessive expense. Donors can suggest a variety of mechanisms for correcting this perceived problem. For example, duplication can be eliminated by combining local or regional operations. In one community in which I interviewed major donors, a respondent advocated the merger of two geographically proximate Jewish federations as a means of cutting costs. He also suggested that "everyone's giving has leveled off. It is going to go down because of the economic conditions in this community. The needs are increasing greatly. What do you do? You don't stick your head in the sand. You've got to address the problem immediately before it happens. If giving is going to be cut to certain causes, tell them now, ahead of time, so they can make their adjustments, but have the foresight to see that happen and make those cuts and adjustments. For example, $200,000 of overhead, whether it is office space, secretarial staff, public relations, mailings, social affairs, all of which if we combined with another federation the costs could be cut by 60 percent or 70 percent just by piggybacking on the other" (Tobin, 1992a).

Major donors view some organizations with large staffs as successful fund raisers and providers of good services. In other cases, large staffs are seen as wasteful. Some smaller organizations are seen as fly-by-night, unstable, and, therefore, untrustworthy. Large organizations mostly have an air of legitimacy—and wastefulness. Small organizations are perceived as frugal, but second-class. The perceptions can also be completely the reverse: an organization so big as to evoke musings that it is not really doing what it is supposed to do, or so small as to evoke musings that all of the money is being pocketed by some unwatched individual.

Some organizations have better images of efficiency than others, yet most of the impressions seem to come from word-of-mouth, rumor, historical perspective, or other general sources. Very few donors actually examine fundraising costs in a serious way. A vague sense of overhead makes donors think about the organization as a whole: "I have my reservations as to the integrity of how the money is allocated, spent, et cetera. I'd rather allocate the money myself than to support what probably is a reasonably worthwhile support staff, a paid group of employees. I remember the cost of fundraising was the least, supposedly the smallest of any major organization. You know, for every dollar you send to the Olympics, 50 cents goes to the desks and 50 cents goes to the athletes. In this organization, supposedly 92 cents goes to the cause and 8 cents goes to fundraising. If that's true, I don't know. I can only take it at face value that it is. I'm not even sure that those statistics are still true" (Tobin, 1989c).

Uncertainty may influence which organizations are chosen and which are not, and how much money is donated, but in indirect and subtle ways, not in some carefully considered analysis of overhead and efficiency. Among donors, levels of knowledge are generally very low about how money is allocated and which services are funded by organizations, particularly by umbrella organizations. Often, this lack of knowledge translates into a sense of waste. Because the donors do not understand exactly how money is spent, or the ways in which donations are used to fund programs, they assume that some of their donation is wasted along the way. "I don't know what the normal services are. But I'm really not that knowledgeable about the organizations they give to, so I'm not an expert on that. And I'm sure there's a big bureaucracy" (Tobin, 1989a). No matter what else this donor knew, he was sure that a big (translated as *too* big) bureaucracy was in place.

Donors use a variety of signs to assess levels of overhead and overall efficiency. On the one hand, organizational offices that are old, crowded, or in disrepair are seen to reflect a second-rate operation. On the other hand, offices that appear *too* nice can be seen as a sign of wasteful overhead. When asked if a particular Jewish organization was efficient or inefficient, one donor in my sample replied, "I don't know. I know they've got fancy new headquarters and normally, when I analyze companies, that's always a sign of decline when they move from an ordinary place into one with polished marble and granite. It's too much money on overhead. That's pretty fancy compared to where they used to be. That's one of the things we always look for when we go into visit a company, whether it's fancy leasehold improvements or fancy moldings, or things like that. If the management is spending too much money on perquisites and not enough on keeping their eye on the fast ball . . ." (Tobin, 1990d). In this case, perceptions of overhead were tied to the physical condition of the offices, which have to have exactly the right balance between a look of competence and a look of thrift.

Greater reliance on volunteers is also seen as a way to reduce overhead. Professional salaries are seen as a fixed expense that goes up constantly, unchecked. One of the means to avoid this problem is through more volunteer help: "Can't a lot be done on a voluntary basis? Can we get someone on a voluntary basis versus a paid person? There are ways that we want to cut and it can be done. People's salaries don't stay the same. Before you know . . . you have a 20 percent or 30 percent overhead increase that you didn't have ten years ago" (Tobin, 1988). Many professionals are seen as unnecessary, especially if the staff seems unrelated to direct fundraising purposes.

Most donors are less likely to understand or want to understand the necessity of investing in fundraising to raise more money. They tend to want to believe that the same amounts of money will be raised regardless of how much is spent. For many, the equation is simple: If a $1 million expenditure on fundraising can raise $20 million (at 10 percent), $500,000 (at 5 percent) can raise the same amount. The opposite view is rarely taken: If a $1 million expenditure raises $10 million, then a $3 million fundraising investment can return $20 million. The percentage may go up to 15 percent, but the net gain is $7 million. Major donors are generally unimpressed with this reasoning and are skeptical about increased returns on fundraising investments.

The nature of the contact between the organization's professionals and a donor has a great deal to do with the donor's perceptions of overhead. Professionals who are viewed as hardworking, competent, and knowledgeable lend credence to the notion that the organization is spending money wisely. Perhaps no indicator influences perceptions of efficiency more than one-on-one contact with the staff. On the other hand, a poor (however judged) staff is definitive proof that the organization is spending too much on administrative overhead. Perceptions of the cost of fundraising, either positive or negative, are also tied to feelings about the lay leadership. If peers or well-respected community citizens are top-level administrators or members of the board, then some major donors assume that the organization is in good hands and therefore well run. If the leadership is unknown to the donors, or disliked, then the donors sometimes assume that the organization is poorly managed. Peer group connections that help a donor understand how the agency works are important for many major donors: "It is very difficult to know what happens to your money in our organization if you don't have some connection to someone who can actually find out for you" (Tobin, 1992b). Therefore, positive or negative perceptions about fundraising are linked to personal contacts with or images of lay leadership, or to feedback from them: "Within each agency it is harder to tell how they spend it, but I think more important than that is the confidence that there is a thoughtful process to allocating the money. I'm not part of that process, but people that I know are" (Tobin, 1993). Or, as one other donor indicated, "I am willing to rely upon the leadership with regard to allocations. They are people that I know and respect, and I am willing to rely upon their decisions" (Tobin, 1992a).

For some major donors, support for the organization is not only an act of trust but also of turning over responsibility because of time constraints, multiple interests, or lack of in-depth interest. Individuals also do not want to feel foolish, misled, or troubled by the possibility that they have donated their money to something wasteful. Therefore, once a major gift is made, the donor would *prefer* to believe that the money is going for the intended purposes and is being used well: "I have enough faith that that agency is run with enough efficiency that the money is used the best that they can. If it is not, I'm not sure that I want to know" (Tobin, 1993).

Donors are concerned about the use of their money and rely on the information given to them by the solicitor. But since annual giving becomes routine for many major donors, they often lose touch with information about fundraising costs on an ongoing basis.

The disagreement about high versus low overhead can be seen in the following focus group discussion (Tobin, 1990b):

MODERATOR: What would you say the percentage is that [Jewish organization] spends on overhead if you were going to estimate?

RESPONDENT 1: I would estimate about 14 percent.

MODERATOR: About 14 percent. How about the rest of you? Any notion, any guess?

RESPONDENT 2: That's just about right and that does not include the overheads of the individual agencies.

MODERATOR: Then you would rank their 14 percent as high?

RESPONDENT 3: Oh, yes.

RESPONDENT 4: I think that if they can do it at 14 percent or 15 percent they are doing darn well.

RESPONDENT 5: I think that's a reasonable percentage, based on what most of the charities do.

RESPONDENT 6: A lot of them are more, but many of them are much less and I think that [Jewish organization] has kind of been creeping up.

Even if there is some agreement about the overhead figure, there is considerable disagreement among donors as to whether or not it is acceptable.

Donors walk a fine line in assessing what are proper expenditures and what are not. For example, most major donors feel that organizations should thank them and other donors properly and make them feel good about the gifts that they are giving. On the other hand, premium gifts, parties, thank-you letters, and too much postage are all construed as signs that the agency may be wasteful: "I think they could do better as positive feedback. I think they could do a better job and could do more of it. I wouldn't want to see them go crazy and create all kinds of vehicles for thank-you's because people at a certain point resent that too, expenditure of dollars raised or charitable, philanthropic purposes spent on parties and thank-you's. On the other hand, I think there's a happy medium" (Tobin, 1992b). The larger the gift, the more likely the donor will be critical of too much mail as unnecessary "stroking" with costly items.

Some donors are actually angry about what they see as mismanagement of the organizations—especially nonprofits—to which they contribute. "When you start dealing with these kinds of nonprofit organization bureaucracies, you are dealing with idiots, number one. Most of them are low paid, so you're dealing with a real double-edged sword. You're dealing with a low-paid guy in a nonprofit organization. Somehow, the fact that it's a nonprofit organization justifies anything he does, which is already stupid. But it makes it palatable because it's a nonprofit organization" (Tobin, 1992b). Although not the norm among the major donors interviewed, the sentiments expressed above were not unique either. Others just assumed that each nonprofit could be better run, by definition, even if it was not terribly mismanaged. When asked to rank the efficiency of an organization, a donor replied, "Again, it's not fair to ask me because I have been out of it for quite some time. I think it's a well-run organization. I think it could be tightened up a little bit" (Tobin, 1992b). Positive images were tempered by the feeling that *something* could be improved because it is a nonprofit organization.

Issues of overhead touch many sensitive areas, including annual gifts, funding of special projects, and establishment of endowment funds. All are interrelated by donors' general feelings of trust and confidence, or of mistrust, in the ability of an organization's administrators to manage resources. Perceptions of excessive overhead are closely linked to other feelings about the organization. Major donors who do not feel highly confident about the agency as a whole are especially reluctant to allow the organization to manage an endowment, even if the donors were willing to match a large annual contribution. For example, one donor was reluctant to create an endowment that was managed by a particular organization because he did not have much faith in the way the organization allocated its annual campaign funds: "I just feel that if it's mishandled at that level, it really isn't handled much better at other levels. I'm not sure I have all that much confidence in the people I've spoken to. But again, it's a personal thing. I think I'd rather just allocate the money myself. I'm not all that impressed with them. It's just the execution seems to be pretty slipshod, and therefore it shakes my confidence and I'd rather turn around and say, 'okay, I'd rather give $10,000 to this, $10,000 to this, $10,000 to this,' and know that that's what I gave and where it went" (Tobin, 1989a). This donor wanted to ensure that he maintained control over his endowment giving.

Another donor discussed the importance of establishing endowments that would be administered by the organization, within the judgment of certain specific individuals:

Nobody has ever come and asked me to give an endowment. I have talked about endowments. I'm talking about unrestricted endowment, not personalized; that's not really endowment. It carries endowment, but it isn't. It's important. We've got to have not only the income to withstand economic shocks but also the income to be able to do those special projects, emergency projects that we otherwise wouldn't be able to afford. So I believe in endowments. You ask me, 'why haven't you come forward? You're somebody who volunteers. You give money without being asked in a lot of places, how come you haven't come forward and given an endowment gift?' I guess the answer to that is that I really hadn't thought about it a lot, and if I thought about it a lot of the things we're doing with our dollars that aren't going into endowment perhaps we and others see as having more of a sense of urgency, more of an immediate impact. I would rather set up a formula by which our assets over a certain number of dollars, when we pass on, that a certain percentage of my estate would go to a foundation. We've set up a charitable foundation. It's an independent foundation. No, independent, and it would be administered by . . . [individual's name] is the sort of person who would be the administrator of it. Now I know that if he were administering the resources that the income would go primarily to my causes because he would know without my telling him that that's where I would want the bulk of the income to go [Tobin, 1992b].

As with many issues of image of the organization, willingness to set up independent endowments depends on personal trust and peer group contacts. Most major donors are unwilling to let organizations manage their funds without some familial or personal contact.

Assessment of the efficiency of an organization is in part based on hope more than knowledge or trust. When asked to rank the quality of an organization to which a major contribution had been made, 10 being the best and 1 the worst, a donor replied, "I would say 7.5 or an 8, I hope. Otherwise I would really feel like a jerk—all that money for nothing!" (Tobin, 1992b). Since decisions to give are largely based on factors other than perceived efficiency of fundraising costs, the donors attempt to match their perceptions with their expectations.

If their faith is betrayed, donors may withdraw. They feel angry and look for other organizations to which to contribute. Generally, they do not stop giving. Their basic assumption is that most organizations are not wasting money unless proven otherwise: "I once gave quite a bit of money to an organization and then found out that they had a 80 percent overhead. I said, 'The hell with you.' Now we give basically to universities for education. We have scholarships in institutions. We do lecture series to raise money for scholarships—that is our primary interest. We do give to other charities" (Tobin, 1988).

Negative news about a particular organization raises some people's suspicions, but generally this does not seriously impact their overall giving. One donor stated, "You know, you also find a lot of skepticism with charitable organizations today. You take the United Way, or you go into UJA [United Jewish Appeal], and there are so many stories on how the money is raised and a large amount goes to fund raisers" (Tobin, 1992a). But these perceptions did not affect this individual's giving patterns at all. The aftermath of a negative scandal about fundraising waste creates a greater demand for more information, but most major donors do not follow up by actually learning more about fundraising costs, even in these circumstances. The relatively minor impact of perceptions of fundraising costs can be traced in part to major donors' general lack of knowledge about the organizations that they support. Most agencies tend to communicate with donors through the mail: solicitations, newsletters, annual reports, brochures, and other mass-produced materials. Overhead costs are usually contained somewhere in these documents, most of which are not read by donors.

Conclusion

Perceptions of fundraising costs are important, but only in the context of many other factors. Perceptions of the organization are more likely to frame feelings and attitudes about fundraising costs than the other way around. When fundraising costs are excessive by some generally understood, if not defined, standard, then this factor can play a primary role in the decision to contribute. But most major-donor concerns about fundraising are intertwined with the overall purpose and image of the organization.

References

Greene, S. G. "Gauging a Charity's Efficiency Can Be Complicated." *Chronicle of Philanthropy,* 1992, 5 (2).

Tobin, G. A. "Focus Group Research Summary of Findings." Unpublished document, prepared for the Jewish Federation of Greater Dallas, Dallas, July 1988.

Tobin, G. A. "Focus Group Analysis." Unpublished document, prepared for the Jewish Federation of South Broward, Hollywood, Fla., Apr. 1989a.

Tobin, G. A. "Focus Group Analysis: Phase 1." Unpublished document, prepared for the United Jewish Federation of MetroWest, East Orange, N.J., Apr. 1989b.

Tobin, G. A. "Focus Group Analysis: Phase 2." Unpublished document, prepared for the United Jewish Federation of MetroWest, East Orange, N.J., May 1989c.

Tobin, G. A. "Focus Group Analysis." Unpublished document, prepared for the Greater Hartford Jewish Federation, Hartford, Conn., Apr. 1990a.

Tobin, G. A. "Focus Group Analysis." Unpublished document, prepared for Combined Jewish Philanthropies of Greater Boston, Boston, Sept. 1990b.

Tobin, G. A. "1990 Marketing Study." Unpublished document, prepared for Greater Hartford Jewish Federation, Hartford, Conn., Oct. 1990c.

Tobin, G. A. "Summary Report, Combined Jewish Philanthropies Marketing Study. Phase 1: Personal Interviews." Unpublished document, prepared for Combined Jewish Philanthropies of Greater Boston, Boston, June 1990d.

Tobin, G. A. "Marketing Study Phase 1: Summary Report." Unpublished document, prepared for the Minneapolis Federation for Jewish Services and the United Jewish Appeal, Minneapolis, Minn., Jan. 1992a.

Tobin, G. A. *Trends in American Jewish Philanthropy: Market Research Analysis.* Policy and Planning Paper No. 8. Waltham, Mass.: Maurice and Marilyn Cohen Center for Modern Jewish Studies, Brandeis University, 1992b.

Tobin, G. A. "Attitudes About Jewish Philanthropy in South Florida." Unpublished document, prepared for the United Jewish Appeal, New York, Apr. 1993.

GARY A. TOBIN *is director of the Maurice and Marilyn Cohen Center for Modern Jewish Studies, Brandeis University, Waltham, Massachusetts.*

National statistics on charitable giving can be very useful, or very harmful to self-evaluation efforts. This chapter alerts us to the pitfalls.

6

Misusing charitable statistics in evaluating fundraising performance

Nathan Weber

DEVELOPMENT OFFICERS, fundraising consultants, and nonprofit directors often cite published statistics on charitable giving as a benchmark to compare their own organizations' performances in raising funds. Typically, a fund raiser or board member for, say, a health association will remark that giving to health nationwide rose X percent last year, while the donations secured for the organization rose by a rate that was higher—or lower, or the same.

Careers can be made or ruined, contracts won or lost, by these extremely misleading comparisons. Those who govern or work for nonprofits should be aware of the purposes and components of charitable statistics, almost all of which are estimates. How are giving estimates derived? What do these estimates really measure, and for which purposes are they valid? And what data can be used appropriately for evaluative comparisons?

These issues are explored in this chapter. But one of the above questions can be answered immediately: For which purposes are the estimates that appear in the periodic yearbooks and compilations valid? They are valid, perhaps invaluable, *only* for the purposes intended: to provide a broad overview of the scope of philanthropic donations, and

NEW DIRECTIONS FOR PHILANTHROPIC FUNDRAISING, NO. 3, SPRING 1994 © JOSSEY-BASS PUBLISHERS

of the general trends and patterns in giving in the United States over the years.

Public perceptions of the estimates

"What happens if you miss one of the canisters? You know, the ones in small stores for Cerebral Palsy?" I was asked this question once, while serving as editor of *Giving USA*. It typifies the way in which many people view the national estimates of philanthropy released each year in that publication. The questioner did not really think that the staff went around to storefronts in all the towns of the United States, counting the pennies dropped into fundraising canisters. But maybe the store owners were required to report them to us?

Behind the question, of course, is the assumption that the data on philanthropic donations represent every dollar—every penny—actually donated. Although the word *estimate* appears before each specific figure, although every estimate is accompanied by a brief statement on how it was derived, and although a more complete description of the estimating methodology appears in an appendix, the belief that the data reflect an actual counting is held tenaciously.

Basic methods: Surveys and formulas

For *Giving USA,* the estimates are derived through two methods: surveys and mathematical formulas. These methods are not mutually exclusive, since most formulas utilize data that are generated by surveys, and all survey data have to be manipulated to some extent mathematically. Still, some of the estimates rely more heavily on the survey component, others on the formulas.

Surveys are conducted by the American Association of Fund-Raising Counsel (AAFRC) Trust for Philanthropy (the publisher of *Giving USA*) and by other national research institutes. For the *Giving USA* surveys, which are sent to organizations in various fields (health, human services, and so on), every nonprofit responding to the questionnaire indicates how much money was received in gifts for the year in question, and for the previous year. The editor sums the reported figures and computes a percentage change between the two years. That percentage difference is then applied to the previous year's published estimate (revised) for that field. The result is the new estimate.

This is the basic survey method. It is used, with variations, to develop estimates of giving to health, human services, the arts, and public and societal benefit (civil rights, government improvement, urban and rural development, and so on). Surveys are also used to compute estimates of the amount of money donated by foundations, corporations, and estates (bequests).

Formulas are employed to derive estimates of giving by individuals, and of giving to education and religion. For the 1991 edition of *Giving USA* (Weber, 1991), formulas were also used to derive first-ever estimates of giving to environmental and international causes, although surveys were employed for these fields as of the 1992 edition.

The most extensive and sophisticated formula utilized by *Giving USA* is the Personal Giving Extrapolation Model (PGEM). Designed solely to estimate the amount of money donated by individuals, this econometric model was developed by Ralph Nelson, a professor of economics at Queens College, City University of New York. It is not discussed in this chapter.

Estimates of giving to health

The estimate for national donations to the health field is based on responses to two surveys: one sent to nonprofit health associations, conducted by the AAFRC Trust, and another sent to nonprofit hospitals, conducted by the Association for Healthcare Philanthropy (AHP). The donations reported in both surveys are added together for each year; a percentage change between the sums for the two surveyed years is computed and used as a proxy for the percentage change in the entire field of health.

What is the problem with this process? Why is it *inexact,* rendering the estimate inappropriate for comparisons to any individual health organization or hospital?

First, at least through the 1991 edition of *Giving USA* (Weber, 1991), the survey of health associations was not based on a random sample, which means the results, strictly speaking, are not generalizable to all health associations in the United States. Certainly, many of the *major* health groups were included (for example, American Heart Association, American Cancer Society, and National Easter Seal Society), as well as a fair number of smaller groups (for example, AirLifeLine, National Psoriasis Foundation, and American Paralysis Association). But only forty-five large and small health groups responded to the survey in 1991 — out of more than thirty-seven thousand health field organizations in the country, according to INDEPENDENT SECTOR (Hodgkinson, Weitzman, Toppe, and Noga, 1992).

Second, the hospital survey conducted by AHP is not a matched sample. The questionnaire requests information solely for the year in question, not for the year before as well. True, the samples are not entirely different, because some of the same hospitals respond each year. But it is highly unlikely that every hospital completing a survey form in one year went through the process the year before, which means the sums from one year to the next are only partially comparable.

Statisticians at AHP deal with this issue through a weighting procedure: the data for the surveyed hospitals are weighted, or statistically expanded, to yield an estimate of donations raised by the total number of hospitals in the AHP membership. This procedure enables them to conclude that each year's report carries an estimate of donations to all the AHP hospitals, so the figures are comparable yearly.

But the weighting procedure reveals a problem of its own, constituting a third source of inexactness in estimates. Only about 400 to 500 hospitals respond each year, out of around 1,400 that are members of AHP. So the survey technicians make the assumption that those who did not respond raised the same amount of funds as those who did respond. That is a large assumption. To be sure, the statisticians first separate out those few hospitals that historically rake in superhigh gifts, so as to keep the bias to a minimum. But after that, they simply multiply the total donations reported by a factor of 3-something: 450-or-so times 3.1 equals around 1,400.

This criticism is not intended to suggest that the process is arbitrary. After years of analyzing income and expense accounts of innumerable hospitals, and evaluating ancillary data that historically affect donations to hospitals (economic cycles, changes in the tax laws, and so forth), the AHP statisticians have reason to believe that their process has merit. We can accept the validity of their process—without denying that the resulting estimates remain "soft."

A fourth factor adds to the inexactness of the national health estimates. The AAFRC Trust survey solicits financial data on a calendar year (CY) basis, or at least that is what the questionnaire stipulates. The AHP data, however, are reported on a fiscal year (FY) basis. To combine data from the two surveys, the AHP figures must be statistically transposed to yield calendar year information. The standard way to do this is to interpolate: Sum the figures for two consecutive fiscal years and divide by two. This produces a calendar year estimate—widely used, acceptable in the best circles, but another step removed from actuality.

Further, interpolation works only so far as the *previous* calendar year, not the current one. Assume, for example, that at the start of 1992, we want to devise estimates for two calendar years: 1990 and 1991. No problem for the earlier year: We simply add the amounts reported in FY 1990 (June 1989–June 1990) and FY 1991 (June 1990–June 1991) and divide the sum by two.

But to develop an estimate for CY 1991, we need data for FY 1992—money raised from June 1991 through June 1992—which does not exist yet. In fact, it will not exist for another six months and probably will not be available for some time after that. So we must take a further step from actuality by devising an estimate within the estimate.

The easiest way is simply to assume that the latest fiscal year data are temporarily the same as the calendar year data. But what this technique gains in simplicity it loses in accuracy, much like painting the oranges red so that they can be added to the apples.

In the past, this was the practice; the resulting estimates were revised the following year, when legitimate interpolated calendar year data became available.

For *Giving USA 1991* (Weber, 1991), a more refined method was employed. Calendar year estimates of AHP donations were devised by averaging the ratio of fiscal-to-calendar-year donations for the past three years, and then applying that ratio to the most current fiscal year donations. This led to the *preliminary* calendar year estimate for hospitals. Of course, the "true"—interpolated—calendar year estimate for 1991 would still have to await the following year's edition, but this method is more valid as an estimating technique than the old way of simply redefining a data set (where one asserts that fiscal data equal calendar data, even though one knows they do not). Were time and money to permit, many refinements to this method could be applied.

Estimates of giving to human services

The procedure for developing the estimates of giving to human services is similar to, but less involved than, that for giving to health. The AAFRC Trust survey of selected human services organizations is combined with an annual survey undertaken by United Way of America. The findings from both surveys are added together, and a percentage change is computed between the combined findings for the current year and those for the previous year. This estimate is less complex to devise because, like the AAFRC Trust survey, the United Way poll is taken on a calendar year basis, so no interpolation, real or estimated, is required. Nevertheless, the problem of inexactness is much the same.

Again, nothing is wrong with any of the above procedures. Given the impossibility of a head count, not to mention the minuscule staff available to produce *Giving USA* under a breakneck deadline, the methods are appropriate for their intended purposes: to arrive at broad estimates of money donated by various sources, and estimates of funds received by various, widely defined fields. The problem arises only when fund raisers assume that these estimates represent hard counts and then proceed to compare them to an individual health organization, hospital, or human services group.

Now, on to the formulas.

Estimates of giving to the environment and international affairs

For the 1991 edition of *Giving USA,* estimates of giving to environmental and international causes were developed for the first time, applied retroactively to 1987. They were made possible by the publication of two biennial studies of individual giving and volunteering, sponsored by INDEPENDENT SECTOR and conducted by the Gallup Organization.

The studies revealed the percentage of household charitable donations made to environmental, international, and other causes in 1987 and 1989. Once the PGEM generated an estimate of individual giving for those years, it was a simple matter to apply the household estimate (using household giving as a proxy for individual giving) to arrive at an estimate of individual giving to the causes. Thus, the PGEM estimate of total giving by individuals in 1989 was $96.78 billion. The INDEPENDENT SECTOR survey showed that household donations to the environment amounted to 1.6 percent of all household charity, or $1.548 billion; and that household donations to international causes amounted to 1.1 percent, or $1.065 billion.

The same process was then used to derive an estimate of foundation and corporate grants to environmental and international organizations. The foundation estimates were based on the annual *Grants Index* published by the Foundation Center (Kovacs, 1990), and the corporate donations relied on unpublished data from an annual survey conducted by The Conference Board (1986). In some instances, the various percentages were adjusted slightly to discount double counting.

After the adjustments were made, the foundation, corporate, and individual estimates were added together to produce the first, or baseline, total estimates in these fields for 1989. Table 6.1 presents the

Table 6.1. Donations to the Environment and International Affairs, 1989

Donation or Grant Source	Total Giving	Percentage to Environment	Giving to Environment	Percentage to International Affairs	Giving to International Affairs
Individuals	$ 96.78	1.6	$1.40	1.1	$1.06
Foundations	6.55	4.9	0.32	3.9	0.21
Corporations	5.60	0.6	0.03	7.97	0.44
Bequests	6.97	NA	NA	NA	NA
Total	$115.90		$1.75		$1.71

Note: Dollar figures are in billions of current dollars. Figures for giving to the environment and giving to international affairs are adjusted. NA = data not available.

Sources: Kovacs, 1990; The Conference Board, 1986; Weber, 1991.

actual computations. For 1988, the method employed interpolated, as opposed to "hard," data for the amount given by individuals. And the 1990 estimates were based on surveys of leading environmental and international affairs organizations: the percentage differences reported by the surveyed groups between 1989 and 1990 were applied to the 1989 estimates (Weber, 1991). (For the 1992 edition of Giving USA, the PGEM estimate of individual giving for 1989 was revised downward and the corporate estimate revised upward, resulting in no change in the originally published 1989 and 1990 environment and international estimates.)

Given the absence of any previous count of dollars raised for the environment and international affairs, this computation method works fine. Nevertheless, some of the same factors rendering the health estimates inexact are at work here as well. Although the survey of household giving utilized a weighted random sample, the data on foundations and corporations were not randomly derived. Further, the corporate figures for giving to international affairs actually reflect a 1986 survey, the last year for which such data had then been collected. The 1988 estimates, again, utilize interpolations. And the 1990 estimates are based on responses to an AAFRC Trust survey by thirty environmental groups out of almost six thousand in the country, and seventeen international affairs groups out of around three thousand (Hodgkinson, Weitzman, Toppe, and Noga, 1992).

A different wrinkle, which affects other estimates as well, is that the Foundation Center's "years" are neither calendar nor fiscal. Rather, they are "composite" years, so what appears as a 1989 figure in fact combines data actually applicable to 1988, 1989, and 1990. This approach is necessary given variations in the reports provided to the center by the nation's grant makers.

Finally, note that the computation does not include any estimate of the amount of money *bequeathed* to environmental or international causes. This may not affect the total seriously, since bequests in the United States tend to go to universities and health and human services organizations. Still, the absence of any bequest figure for the computations may contribute further to the inexact nature of the resulting estimates.

Estimates of giving to religion and to education

What is true for estimates of giving to the environment and to international affairs applies to the estimates of giving to religion and to education. Since a survey of religious organizations would be extremely difficult to undertake, given the plethora of religions in the United States, the estimate (as of the 1991 edition of *Giving USA*) relies entirely on formulas. The INDEPENDENT SECTOR survey revealed that 64.5 percent of household donations went to religion in 1989. The *Grants Index* (Kovacs, 1990) reported that 1.4 percent of foundation grants went to religion that (composite) year. Virtually no corporations give money for religion, and we have no information on religious bequests, so the estimate in Weber (1991) is based solely on data for donations by individuals and foundations. Obviously, the resulting figure of $62.51 billion—a 7.6 percent increase over the 1988 estimate—has little relevance to any single church, synagogue, mosque, temple, or other house of worship, at least for the purpose of evaluative comparisons.

The estimate of giving to education in Weber (1991) was derived from a different, more complex formula, but the issue of inexactness obtains here as well. The algebraic equation employs data, also estimates, from an annual survey of gifts to institutions of higher learning and to selected secondary schools, conducted by the Council for Aid to Education (CFAE, 1991b). That survey provides a breakdown of donors by type—foundations, business, and individuals (alumni and others). Other sources include the CFAE (1991a) report of corporate donations, and the Foundation Center's *Grants Index*.

It is not necessary to list the specific mathematical steps here; they entail, among other things, converting the source data from fiscal (or "academic") years to interpolated calendar years, and devising a simple formula for individual giving to secondary schools. As in the case of health, these steps necessarily detract from the actuality of the education estimate. But one additional factor, having more to do with definitions than with mathematics, reinforces the problem.

CFAE provides an estimate of total foundation giving to higher education, and the *Grants Index* provides data on the proportion of foundations' education grants allocated to both higher and nonhigher education. With these figures, it is a straightforward matter to compute total foundation giving to education, one component of the final education estimate.

Although straightforward, the computation of total foundation giving to education is problematic. The definition of higher education varies from CFAE to the Foundation Center. CFAE considers a gift to any unit within a university as a higher education gift. Not so the Foundation Center. It defines a gift to, say, a university arts center as a donation to the arts, not education. At present, there is little likelihood that these definitions will be harmonized.

Finally, with the publication of the 1992 edition of *Giving USA* (Kaplan, 1992), it appears that the above formula has been simplified, so that the estimates for giving to education are now based *solely* on changes in estimates to *higher* education—yet another move away from actuality.

Nonprofit Almanac 1992–93:
Dimensions of the Independent Sector

The cumulative data in Hodgkinson, Weitzman, Toppe, and Noga (1992) are also not very appropriate for individual fundraising comparisons. Data from the *Nonprofit Almanac 1992–93* are based on 501(c)(3) organizations reporting mainly for 1987 and 1989 to the Internal Revenue Service, which means that most of the information is now several years out of date. Changes in our economic environment since then have undoubtedly affected the financial status of the individual groups.

More important, the data are cumulative, reflecting thousands of organizations within each field, from the very large to the very small; the volume does not offer income breakdowns by organizational size. The long-awaited directory of facts and figures within the volume provides a wealth of information heretofore unavailable, but the numbers have little relevance to the evaluation of fundraising performance.

Sources for valid comparisons

If it is invalid to cite the broad national estimates to compare any individual organization's accomplishments, what data can be used appropriately? Probably the most useful comparisons are to be made against the figures reported by specific individual organizations, or by groups of organizations that are truly comparable to one's own. Selection of the measures of comparability is, of course, a management responsibility. Typical measures include asset or income size, type of service provision, location, institutional history, number of employees, earned-income-to-debt ratio, and a host of other items. Once these components are determined, comparable organizations can be pinpointed, and their own fundraising figures used as criteria.

Incidentally, comparison with other nonprofits, even those that are similar to one's own, is hardly the only valid evaluative criterion. This obvious fact often gets lost in our culture of competition. Comparison with the *fundraising history* of the nonprofit for which one works is equally appropriate, as are measurements of funds raised against goals set by the board, or even against lesser goals needed to realistically accomplish institutional projects, such as capital construction and creation of a scholarship endowment.

But if competitive comparisons are desired, valid sources do exist. The *Chronicle of Philanthropy* now annually publishes the amount of donations received by the four hundred largest cnaritable organizations. Development officers might scan the list to select only those charities that are appropriate as models or competitors. A similar service had been provided in *Giving USA* up through the 1991 edition; that list, which included small as well as large groups, also separated bequests from total funds raised for groups in health and human services. Although *Giving USA* has since discontinued its listing, back issues may be available for historical comparisons.

CFAE, again, publishes an annual report listing donations to hundreds of specific colleges and universities. Similar information in other fields may be obtainable through professional and trade associations, or research institutes. The National Wildlife Federation, for instance, publishes an annual directory of environmental and animal-related organizations. While it does not offer financial data, the directory simplifies the task of contacting the individual organizations for copies of their annual reports, each of which usually provides a breakout of donated income. And, of course, there is the multivolume *Encyclopedia of Associations,* which provides basic information on numerous organizations in every field.

Religious fund raisers may find useful data in the *Yearbook of American and Canadian Churches,* which lists the amount of donations received by major Protestant congregations in the United States and Canada. Jewish and Catholic associations, such as the Council of Jewish Federations in New York and the National Catholic Development Conference on Long Island, may provide leads to fundraising performance within those respective religions. Little published data exist on

Islam in the United States, but several Islamic institutes may offer helpful insights on aspects of Islamic philanthropy.

Do-it-yourself statistics

Fund raisers can also develop their own, more appropriate cumulative
figures, including averages and percentage changes. Many development officers have sharpened their data collection skills while preparing feasibility studies. Those skills can be employed as well for
evaluation.

The National Center for Charitable Statistics, an arm of INDEPEN-
DENT SECTOR, now provides labels of organizations within all fields
classified according to the National Taxonomy of Exempt Entities—
the classification system used by *Giving USA,* the Foundation Center,
and other statistics-generating institutions. The labels are comparable
in cost to those charged by commercial list brokers and can be ordered,
randomly or otherwise, according to organizational income, asset
range, geography, and other criteria.

With the labels in hand, it is not difficult to mail brief survey forms
to gather fundraising data from the exact type or types of organization
specified. (One suggestion: keep the form *very* brief; peers are likely to
be busy and to look askance at spending too much time on a questionnaire.) Organizations lacking staff expertise in conducting surveys
may find assistance from local universities, or from independent research consultants. Once the returns are in, they will comprise an excellent data base of relevant information on which to develop
evaluative comparisons.

References

The Conference Board. "Survey of Corporate Contributions." Unpublished data,
The Conference Board, New York, 1986.
Council for Aid to Education (CFAE). *Corporate Support of Education.* New York:
Council for Aid to Education, 1991a.

Council for Aid to Education. *Voluntary Support of Education, 1990.* New York: Council for Aid to Education, 1991b.

Hodgkinson, V. A., and Weitzman, M. S. (eds.). "Giving and Volunteering in the United States: Findings from a National Survey." Washington, D.C.: INDEPENDENT SECTOR, 1992.

Hodgkinson, V. A., Weitzman, M. S., Toppe, C. M., and Noga, S. M. (eds.). *Nonprofit Almanac 1992–93: Dimensions of the Independent Sector.* San Francisco: Jossey-Bass, 1992.

Kaplan, A. E. (ed.). *Giving USA 1992.* New York: American Association of Fund-Raising Counsel Trust for Philanthropy, 1992.

Kovacs, R. (ed.). *Grants Index.* (19th ed.) New York: Foundation Center, 1990.

Weber, N. (ed.). *Giving USA 1991.* New York: American Association of Fund-Raising Counsel Trust for Philanthropy, 1991.

NATHAN WEBER *is founder and president of Weber Reports, an economic research and editorial services firm in New York City. He is former editor of* Giving USA *and a former senior research associate for The Conference Board, a business and economic research organization.*

*This chapter explores the development of state regu-
lation of fundraising for charity. The author explains
why regulation has not worked as it should and suggests measures that will strengthen regulatory efforts
without further burdening charities.*

7

Government regulation of fundraising:
A struggle for efficacy

David E. Ormstedt

THE REGULATION of fundraising by state governments is controversial.
It is not so much the concept of regulation that is problematic to charities but rather the manner in which states have carried it out. In this
chapter, I briefly explore the development of state regulation and some
of the key issues affecting it. My primary goals are to explain why state
regulation has not worked as it should and to suggest measures that
states can take to strengthen regulatory efforts while preserving the vi-
tality of charitable institutions.

Origin, development, and deficiencies of regulation

In most states, it is a fundamental principle of common law that the
attorney general has visitation rights upon charities to ensure the due
application of charitable assets. In states without such a common law
tradition, statutes have been enacted granting the state attorney general that authority (Ross, 1990). The rationale lies in the attorney

NEW DIRECTIONS FOR PHILANTHROPIC FUNDRAISING, NO. 3, SPRING 1994 © JOSSEY-BASS PUBLISHERS

general's role as the legal representative of the community. Gifts for charitable purposes benefit society and should be encouraged and protected. The community, represented by its attorney, should be able to enforce the proper use of those gifts (Scott and Fratcher, 1989).

Following World War II, fundraising for charitable purposes proliferated, and with it came well-publicized scandals. The publicity led to calls for legislation to more closely regulate charities (Hopkins, 1991). To strengthen public confidence in charities and to ward off unwise legislation, the National Health Council, a coalition of national health charities, drafted model state solicitation law provisions, which it urged states considering legislation to adopt (National Health Council, 1965). The laws that emerged required most soliciting charities to register and file annual financial reports with the state. They also regulated the fundraising process.

The rationale for early state legislation was that sunshine would cure all evils. That is, if soliciting charities were required to register and annually file financial reports with the state, the public would be able to use those reports to distinguish the worthy from the unworthy. True charity would thrive while the fraudulent would wither on the vine from lack of financial support. The rationale proved more myth than reality. Indeed, the way in which the system came to operate tended to be more onerous on the compliant agencies than on the miscreants that the system was supposed to expose. The well-intentioned in general dutifully registered and filed their financial reports. Others simply ignored the law and registered only when a state caught up with them. Moreover, those charities that registered and filed their reports sometimes found themselves, ironically, to be the ones questioned by the regulators.

This less than ideal situation became worse when states enacted laws limiting the amount a charity could spend to raise funds. In some states, the limit was expressed as a percentage of all contributions or revenue. Other states only limited amounts paid to professional fund raisers (Quandt, 1975). With these laws, some charities faced the prospect of having their right to solicit in one or more states terminated because their fundraising costs exceeded an arbitrary limit set by the state.

It is here that accounting rules became inextricably intertwined with the law. The National Health Council and the National Assembly for Social Policy and Development (1964), in publishing accounting standards for health and welfare charities, attempted to counter the same criticism that had led to the enactment of state charitable solicitation laws. Known as the "Black Book" because of the appearance of its cover, the standards expressed a conservative approach to allocating between program and fundraising the costs associated with an activity that had elements of both. For example, if a mailing included program information but the primary purpose of the mailing was to raise funds, then, according to the standards, all costs of the mailing were to be charged to fundraising. The exception to the rule was that the incremental cost of a separate program piece included with the mailing could be charged to the program. Strict application of this accounting standard caused some charities to report fundraising costs in excess of the legal limits, jeopardizing their reputations and right to solicit.

If the fundraising law limits could not be changed, the next best strategy was to change how fundraising costs were calculated. Since the fundraising percentage is determined by dividing fundraising expenses by total contributions, the percentage can be altered by changing the numerator. That is precisely what was accomplished when the American Institute of Certified Public Accountants promulgated Statement of Position No. 78-10, later amended with cosmetic changes as No. 87-2 (American Institute of Certified Public Accountants, 1978, 1987). It permits charities to liberally allocate the costs of an activity between fundraising and program. Almost always, the program allegedly accomplished is education of the public. Thus, what heretofore had been fundraising costs now became program expenses. For many charities, especially those delivering little or nothing in the way of tangible services, the new rule of accounting resulted in a lower fundraising-to-revenue ratio and, conversely, a higher program-to-revenue ratio. That change not only virtually eliminated the threat of state sanctions for having high fundraising costs but also improved the image of the charity as seen through its state and general purpose financial reports.

As it turned out, the threat of prosecution for violating fundraising expense limits was temporary. In 1980, the U.S. Supreme Court in *Village of Schaumburg v. Citizens for a Better Environment* (444 U.S. 620) ruled that fundraising was speech fully protected by the First Amendment and, therefore, could not be restricted by government without a compelling interest and then only by the most narrowly tailored of means. It was the court's opinion that the act of fundraising is so linked to the dissemination and advocacy of ideas that regulation of the former invariably impinges on the latter. In so holding, the court struck down a municipal ordinance that imposed a 25 percent ceiling on fundraising expenses. In 1984, the Supreme Court in *Secretary of State of Maryland v. Joseph H. Munson, Co.* (467 U.S. 947) clarified and expanded its ruling, holding that a state law that only restricted the amount that a charity could pay to a professional fund raiser, in contrast to the amount a charity could spend on fundraising in general, was no less constitutionally defective.

Even before the 1984 Supreme Court decision, there was a perception among some state regulatory officials that a new approach was needed to the regulation of charitable solicitations. Under the auspices of the National Association of Attorneys General Charitable Trusts and Solicitations Committee, a joint state and private sector committee drafted a model charitable solicitation statute, which was completed in 1986 (Ormstedt, 1989). The document failed to achieve widespread acceptance for two principal reasons.

First, the document failed to address the issue of uniformity in filing and financial reporting. Many national charities wanted to be relieved of what they saw as a burden in completing up to forty different registration and annual report forms. While the revision of the Internal Revenue Service (IRS) Form 990 a few years earlier to make it suitable as a common federal and state reporting form had brought some degree of uniformity, there was still a long way to go. The model law did not address that concern and, therefore, was viewed as inconsequential by many.

Second, what many regulators saw as the key feature of the model law was virtually stillborn. Disclosure to donors by paid solicitors of the amount of the contributions that would actually go to charity (the inverse of the costs of raising the donations) was seen by many regulators as the critically needed alternative to the fundraising limitation struck down by the Supreme Court. However, in April 1987, less than five months after the attorneys general ratified the model law, the U.S. Fourth Circuit Court of Appeals affirmed a federal district court decision declaring unconstitutional a similar provision of a North Carolina law. Fourteen months later, in 1988, the U.S. Supreme Court in *Riley v. National Federation of the Blind* (487 U.S. 781) affirmed the findings of the lower courts.

To be sure, the model law comprised more than the defective disclosure requirement. For example, the distinction it draws between fundraising counsel and professional solicitor is viewed by many as a desirable feature. Nevertheless, the U.S. Supreme Court decision is viewed as having discredited the model. Although a few states still looked to the model for guidance in amending existing or enacting new laws, many states began individual quests for legislation best suited to them.

The legislative activity is a two-edged sword. On the one hand, states are serving as testing grounds for new ideas in solicitation regulation. It is possible that one statute, or elements of several statutes, will prove to be successful in controlling the abusive activity while not unduly burdening charity. On the other hand, this legislative activity may produce disparate regulatory requirements that will confuse and further burden national charities.

Identifying regulatory objectives

State regulators and charities alike must reexamine regulation of charitable solicitation. There is a need for states to exercise their police power in this area. However, it is obvious that the current regulatory scheme is not optimal. The primary reasons for this are that, first, there is no regulatory mission statement to guide states in the development and execution of their programs; second, resources allocated to state regulatory agencies are inadequate; and, third, tension and mistrust exists between regulators and the charitable sector, inhibiting the co-operation necessary for the development of a consensus that effective regulation of fraud is in the best interest of charity and the public.

The creation of a regulatory mission statement starts with identification of the public interests at stake. First, the charitable sector, including our national tradition of philanthropy and volunteering, must be strong. It is unnecessary to reiterate here the value of charitable organizations to this nation and its society. Government serves its citizens well when it permits organizations that serve the public benefit to carry out their missions unimpeded by unreasonable regulation. This is not to say that government should permit anyone claiming to be charitable to operate with a free hand, for much fraud on the public is committed in the name of charity. It does mean that in the legitimate quest to prosecute and deter fraud, government must avoid a heavy-handed approach that burdens legitimate charity.

Second, Americans need to have confidence in their charitable institutions. Charities exist to serve the public trust and depend on the public trust for their existence. Government should do what it can to foster public trust in and encourage giving to charitable institutions.

Third, to maintain a strong charitable sector and to foster confidence in charitable institutions, fraud in the name of charity must be minimized. The public needs reasonable assurance that their donations, as well as their tax dollars used to subsidize charities, are being applied in a manner consistent with their expectations. Thus, government needs to be able and prepared to ensure the due application of charitable funds. This means not only prosecuting fraud but also ensuring that restricted donations are used for the restricted purpose. A person who donates money in response to an appeal for money for financial assistance to victims of a disease has every right to expect that the donation will be used for that purpose and not some other purpose, even if the alternate purpose serves a charitable objective.

Fourth, the public needs accurate and usable information about individual charities. Americans should donate to charitable causes. Yet Americans should not be asked to give their money and time to charity blindly. The public should have access to accurate information in a form usable to them that will enable informed giving.

Fifth, the public needs accurate aggregate information on the entire charitable sector. Despite the great strides in recent years in publishing comprehensive data on the sector, it is far from clear that the public and the policymakers in government understand the full scope of the sector and its contributions to the welfare of our society. More specifically, the data could yield comprehensive information as to where and for what purposes charities are allocating their resources (Hodgkinson, Weitzman, Toppe, and Noga, 1992).

Having identified the goals of regulation, we must recognize the constraints on the accomplishment of those goals: (1) There will always be fraud and other misuse of charitable assets. There is fraud and abusive conduct in every segment of society. Government cannot eradicate it. The best government can hope for, and the most the public should expect of government, is that efficient regulation will keep problems reasonably under control. (2) The size and diversity of the charitable sector are so great that it is difficult to devise a "one-size-fits-all" regulatory scheme. (3) Considerable fundraising and program activities of charities are conducted nationally and internationally, thus limiting individual state jurisdiction and access to information. (4) States will likely continue to have relatively few resources to devote to the regulation of charitable solicitations. Currently, a minority of states have the resources necessary to fully accomplish the objectives. While a large bureaucracy is not needed, a commitment of adequate resources is necessary. States not willing or able to devote necessary resources should not require charities to register and report. If the states cannot put to good use the information they receive, they should not ask the charities to provide it.

Recommended guidelines for regulation

The suggested regulatory model that flows from close observance of the objectives and constraints discussed above contains elements of current state requirements. However, it calls on states to alter the manner in which they apply those elements. The following is not intended as a detailed description of what should be contained in a state law regulating charitable solicitation. Rather, it is intended as a discussion of the philosophical principles that should guide states as they develop and implement regulatory programs.

A regulatory program should encompass all organizations that receive and hold assets for the public benefit. Most programs currently focus on soliciting charities and social welfare organizations only, groups that generally are exempt from federal taxation pursuant to sections 501(c)(3) and (c)(4) of the Internal Revenue Code and that derive support principally by fundraising from the general public. There are, however, other classes of organizations that serve or purport to serve the public good. For example, police and firefighter unions and fraternal associations typically solicit the public for contributions that will allegedly be used for charitable purposes, such as scholarships and youth athletic programs. The regulatory program should treat similarly all organizations that ask the public for donations or in-kind support, which each organization represents will be used for the public benefit.

Regulation of private foundations should be integrated with regulation of public charities. A minority of states currently have oversight programs with respect to private foundations. Among some of them, the program resides in the Attorney General's Office while the regulation of soliciting charities resides in another state agency (Ross, 1990). Regulatory economy in the accomplishment of program objectives requires that the functions be merged.

States should require all organizations soliciting, receiving, or holding assets for the public benefit to register. It is important to distinguish between licensing and registration. Licensing implies state analysis of the organization's qualifications or fitness and is of questionable constitutionality. Registration serves merely to announce that the organization will be soliciting and provides the state with basic information about the nature of the organization. Registration should be a universal requirement. All organizations, except for those with limited revenue and assets, should file periodic financial reports.

State financial reporting requirements are what fuel the debate over regulation. Few organizations are directly touched by state prosecutorial activity. However, most organizations feel the impact of the financial reporting obligation, particularly national organizations that must now report in over forty states.

Although organizations generally do not quarrel with the concept of reporting, some have a serious problem with the way in which the requirement is implemented. They complain that a lack of uniformity among states with respect to their forms, filing dates, supplemental schedules, and levels of detail required imposes a financial burden on them that necessarily detracts from their ability to carry out their program services. The number of organizations adversely affected is small relative to the total number of reporting organizations. Moreover, reasonable minds can differ about the extent to which charities are adversely affected. Nevertheless, the controversy over the various state reporting requirements, a controversy that permeates the discussion about regulation and polarizes the participants, is unnecessary.

States can and should quell the debate by asking only for information that they and the public can reasonably and routinely use. IRS Form 990 and its required schedules provide virtually all of the information that states routinely need from charities. Whatever else the states think they need can be supplied on a supplement that should not exceed two pages. The supplement could readily double as the reregistration form in those states with annual registrations.

There should be uniformity among the states in what is required and when it is required. Experience demonstrates that is easier said than done. The more information each state thinks it needs, the less likely forty states can agree on a common format. If states limited the information routinely required of filers, the prospects for uniformity would be enhanced. With respect to due dates, there seems little reason why the IRS deadline of four and one-half months could not serve as the national standard.

On those occasions when a state needs additional information in pursuit of an investigation, investigative subpoenas and other, similar tools should be available and used. There are practical and legal constraints on the ability of states to compel production of documents and testimony from persons and entities beyond a state's border. Nevertheless, it is better to live with those constraints than to require all charities to routinely file voluminous material for which the states will have only an occasional need.

Having required charities to file financial reports, states should do something constructive with the data. IRS Form 990 offers very good information, provided charities fill it out correctly. States should keypunch into a computer as much data as possible, which should be available to the general public, researchers, scholars, legislators, and others interested in nonprofits. Using the National Taxonomy of Exempt Entities, a classification system for nonprofit organizations, states can provide an array of useful information about the charitable sector and its constituent parts (Hodgkinson, Weitzman, Toppe, and Noga, 1992).

Aside from registration and reporting issues, the issue that most concerns states and charities alike is what information states should require charities to disclose to potential donors. While the Supreme Court in *Riley* enunciated the constitutional limits on mandated point-of-solicitation disclosure, that same decision made it clear that disclosure requirements are not *per se* unlawful. Thus, some states require charities to disclose information that is believed to be important to donors. The disclosures include whether contributions are tax deductible, whether the solicitation is being made by a professional fund raiser, the purpose for which the funds will be used, and the name and address of the state agency from which persons can obtain information about the charity.

It is important for donors to have useful information about a charity at the time they are making a decision about whether to give. But too much information can be confusing to donors and arranged by charities so as to obfuscate rather than inform. States, when deciding what information they think their citizens need, should consider the consequences of potentially forty states requiring several disclosures in various formats. For example, several states require that charities include in solicitation material the name and address of the state agency from which information about the charity may be obtained. That information may be useful to potential donors and not burdensome for charities soliciting in only one or two states. A different result is attained when the solicitation is mailed throughout the country and forty states require publication of an agency's name, address, and sundry other information.

States need to set administrative and enforcement priorities. There are significant problems in charitable fundraising and the administration of charitable assets. States cannot adequately address the problems if they occupy their time struggling with charities to get information that will ultimately be of little value to them. The following are suggested areas of pervasive interest to the states.

First, states should ensure that charities file accurate financial information. Financial reporting by charities is dangerously close to unreliability and, therefore, uselessness. The problems are significant and include unreasonable allocations of fundraising and management expenses to program, arithmetic errors, inaccurate reporting of contributions, inaccurate reporting of expenses, and gross overvaluation of in-kind contributions received and grants made.

Second, misrepresentations made during the course of fundraising are far from unusual. They include misrepresentation of the purpose for which funds are being raised, exaggeration or fabrication of past performance, and professional solicitors passing themselves off as charity volunteers.

Third, waste and misuse of charitable assets should be pursued. Self-dealing by charity trustees, directors, and staff, use of restricted assets for other purposes, and participation in financial transactions that jeopardize the ability of the charity to carry out its mission are all important areas of concern.

While states can do much to improve the efficacy of fundraising regulation, the private sector also has an unfulfilled responsibility. Charities cannot act as though oblivious to the problems that exist. In the long run, public confidence in charitable institutions will erode. As a society, we cannot afford to let that happen. It is not that charities should be policemen. They should, however, take steps to help enable the public to distinguish the wheat from the chaff. These steps may include the following.

First, meaningful codes of ethics and other self-regulatory measures must be established. Existing codes are sometimes more form than substance. Strong standards of conduct, which are actually enforced against violators, would constitute a positive step.

Second, private sector leaders must speak out against fraud and abuse. Too often, the reaction of sector leaders to reports of problems is silence, avoidance, or denial. None of these reactions best serves the interests of charity. The public needs to hear from respected leaders in philanthropy that fraudulent charitable activity is the exception and is intolerable.

Third, charitable organizations must undertake public education efforts. The public and the media both need a better understanding of the realities of fundraising. If charities talked about fundraising costs, why it costs money to raise money, and what are reasonable fundraising costs, perhaps people would be less shocked when they discover that less than all of their contributions are used for programs. It is even possible that greater public awareness will reduce the need for charities to use creative accounting techniques.

Conclusion

Implementation of these recommendations nationwide will take time. In some states, legislative amendments will be required. As mentioned, few states at present have adequate staff resources. Only a handful of states have computer technology dedicated to charity regulation; that situation will need to change if states are to take advantage of the information in their files. The charitable sector has been slow to do its part. But we need to start somewhere. If a few states take the lead, efficient and effective regulation may eventually become a reality.

References

American Institute of Certified Public Accountants (AICPA). *Accounting Principles and Reporting Practices for Certain Nonprofit Organizations.* Statement of Position No. 78-10. New York: AICPA, 1978.

American Institute of Certified Public Accountants. *Audits of Certain Nonprofit Organizations.* New York: AICPA, 1981.

American Institute of Certified Public Accountants. *Accounting for Joint Costs of Informational Materials and Activities of Not-for-Profit Organizations That Include a Fund-Raising Appeal.* Statement of Position No. 87-2. New York: AICPA, 1987.

Hodgkinson, V. A., Weitzman, M. S., Toppe, C. M., and Noga, S. M. (eds.). *Nonprofit Almanac 1992–93: Dimensions of the Independent Sector.* San Francisco: Jossey-Bass, 1992.

Hopkins, B. R. *The Law of Fund-Raising.* New York: Wiley, 1991.

National Health Council. *Viewpoints: State Legislation Regulating Solicitation of Funds from the Public.* New York: National Health Council, 1965.

National Health Council, and National Assembly for Social Policy and Development. *Standards of Accounting and Financial Reporting for Voluntary Health and Welfare Organizations.* New York: National Health Council, 1964.

Ormstedt, D. "State Authority to Regulate Charitable Solicitation." In D. Kurtz and J. Small (eds.), *Nonprofit Organizations 1989: Current Issues and Developments.* New York: Practising Law Institute, 1989.

Quandt, K. "The Regulation of Charitable Fundraising and Spending Activities." *Wisconsin Law Review, 1975, 1975,* 1158.

Ross, L. M. (ed.). *State Attorneys General: Power and Responsibilities.* Washington, D.C.: Bureau of National Affairs, 1990.

Scott, A. W., and Fratcher, W. F. *The Law of Trusts.* (4th ed.) Boston: Little, Brown, 1989.

DAVID E. ORMSTEDT *is assistant attorney general and head of the Public Charities Unit in the Office of the Connecticut Attorney General, Hartford.*

Additional Resources

Berendt, R. J., and Taft, J. R. *How to Rate Your Development Department.* Washington, D.C.: Taft Group, 1984.

Blazek, J. *Tax and Financial Planning for Tax-Exempt Organizations.* New York: Wiley, 1990.

Council for Advancement and Support of Education and National Association of College and University Business Officers. *Expenditures in Fund Raising, Alumni Relations, and Other Constituent (Public) Relations.* Washington, D.C.: Council for Advancement and Support of Education, 1990.

Drucker, P. F. *Managing the Nonprofit Organization: Practices and Principles.* New York: HarperCollins, 1990.

Fink, N. S., and Metzler, H. C. *The Costs and Benefits of Deferred Giving.* New York: Columbia University Press, 1982.

Greenfield, J. M. "Fund-Raising Costs and Credibility: What the Public Wants to Know." *National Society of Fund Raising Executives Journal,* Autumn 1988, pp. 46–53.

Gross, K. S. "Managing for Results." In H. A. Rosso and Associates, *Achieving Excellence in Fund Raising: A Comprehensive Guide to Principles, Strategies, and Methods.* San Francisco: Jossey-Bass, 1991.

Gross, M. J., Jr., Washauer, W., Jr., and Larkin, R. F. *Financial and Accounting Guide for Not-for-Profit Organizations.* (4th ed.) New York: Wiley, 1991.

Harr, D. J., Godfrey, J. T., and Frank, R. H. "Are Volunteers Worth Their Weight in Gold, but Not in Dollars?" *Philanthropy Monthly,* Sept. 1992, pp. 12–27.

Hopkins, B. R. *The Law of Tax-Exempt Organizations.* (6th ed.) New York: Wiley, 1991.

Hopkins, B. R. *Starting and Managing a Nonprofit Organization: A Legal Guide.* (2nd ed.) New York: Wiley, 1993a.

Hopkins, B. R. *The Tax Law of Charitable Giving.* New York: Wiley, 1993b.

Howe, F. *The Board Member's Guide to Fund Raising: What Every Trustee Needs to Know About Raising Money.* San Francisco: Jossey-Bass, 1991.

Internal Revenue Service Form 990, Schedule A, and Instructions. Washington, D.C.: Government Printing Office, 1992.

Jacobson, H. J. "Fifteen Ways to Measure Fund Raising Program Effectiveness." *Fund Raising Management,* Dec. 1982.

Khalaf, R. "The Accounting Games Charities Play." *Forbes,* Aug. 26, 1992a, pp. 252–254.

Khalaf, R. "Evaluating Fundraising Efficiency." *Forbes,* Aug. 26, 1992b, pp. 256–258.

Murray, D. J. *Evaluation of Fund Raising Programs: A Management Audit Approach.* Boston: American Institute of Management, 1983.

Murray, D. J. *The Guaranteed Fund-Raising System: A Systems Approach to Planning and Controlling Fund Raising.* Poughkeepsie, N.Y.: American Institute of Management, 1987.

National Charities Information Bureau. *Grantmakers Guide to a New Tool for Philanthropy: Form 990.* New York: National Charities Information Bureau, 1983.

New, A. L., and Levis, W. C. *Raise More Money for Your Nonprofit Organization.* New York: Foundation Center, 1991.

O'Connell, B. *Budgeting and Financial Accountability.* Washington, D.C.: INDEPENDENT SECTOR, 1988.

Weinstein, S. "Time Management and the Development Professional." *National Society of Fund Raising Executives Journal,* Winter 1991, pp. 42–53.

Index

Internal Revenue Service, data from, 125
International giving, comparative statistics for, 121–123
IRS Form 8283, 35–36
IRS Form 990, 42, 132, 137, 138
Islamic philanthropy, 127

Jewish philanthropists, 95–113; fundraising efforts towards, 95–101; perceptions of fundraising costs, 101–112
Joint costs, 44–45

Kaplan, A. E., 124, 128
Kovacs, R., 121, 123, 128

Larkin, R. F., 2, 17, 27, 54, 88, 89, 90
Leslie, J. W., 81, 92
Leslie, L. L., 81, 92
Lindahl, W. E., 3, 17, 19, 30, 67, 77, 83, 84, 85, 92
Linear regression projection, 78–80
Loans, 11–12
Loessin, B. A., 81–82, 92
Long-range vs. cash-only investment, 51, 52
Lotus 1-2-3, 79, 88

Madsen, R. W., 78, 93
Major donors: allocation by, 110–111; attitudes of, towards fundraising costs, 101–112; cost assessment by, 106–107; and direct mail, 98–99, 109; and endowments, 110, 111; Jewish, 95–98; and mismanagement, 109–110; motives of, 3, 96–97; multiyear evaluation of, 85–86; and peer group connections, 108; personal contact with, 99–100, 107–108, 111; positive feedback to, 100, 103, 109; and premiums, 109; project orientation of, 98; and solicitors, 100–101, 104; volunteerism among, 97, 98. See also Donor decisions
Major gifts: competition for, 96; forecasting revenues from, 68; multiyear evaluation of, 85–86; time delay in, 84–85
Marginal returns, 15–17, 18; averaging of, 20–21; estimating of, 21–22
Maximization, 15
Maximum willingness to pay, 17–19

Measurement tools, 3; criteria for, 55–69; implementation of, 74–75; practical utility of, 49–55. See also Productivity and efficiency analysis
Merging, of nonprofit organizations, 105
Minimization, 15
Moeschberger, M. L., 78, 93
Moore, M. E., 75, 76
Moral obligation, as donor motive, 96–97
Moving averages, 79, 80
Multiyear performance evaluation, 67, 77; and development effort, 81–84; development report for, 87–92; and organizational goals, 86–87; projection techniques for, 78–81; and time delays, 84–86
Murray, D., 85, 93

Nalebuff, B. J., 12, 24
National Assembly for Social Policy and Development, 131, 141
National Association of Attorneys General Charitable Trusts and Solicitations Committee, 132
National Association of College and University Business Officers (NACUBO), 71, 75, 81, 88, 92
National Catholic Development Conference, 126
National Center for Charitable Statistics, 127
National Easter Seal Society, 118
National Health Council, 130, 131, 141
National Psoriasis Foundation, 118
National statistics, as evaluation tool, 4. See also Comparative statistics
National Taxonomy of Exempt Entities, 127, 138
National Wildlife Federation, 126
Nelson, R., 117
Net benefit, 17–18
New-donor club, 71
Noga, S. M., 118, 123, 125, 128, 135, 138, 141
Noncash gifts, accounting for, 34–38
Nonprofit Almanac, 4, 125
Northwestern University, 80–81, 83, 84, 85–87, 90, 91

Optimization, 2, 9–17; of donor decisions, 22–24; of fundraising, 9–12;

Ordering Information

NEW DIRECTIONS FOR PHILANTHROPIC FUNDRAISING is published quarterly in Fall, Winter, Spring, and Summer and available for purchase by subscription and individually.

SUBSCRIPTIONS for 1993–94 cost $59.00 for individuals (a savings of 35 percent over single-copy prices) and $79.00 for institutions, agencies, and libraries. Please do not send institutional checks for personal subscriptions. Standing orders are accepted.

SINGLE COPIES cost $19.95 when payment accompanies order. (California, New Jersey, New York, and Washington, D.C., residents please include appropriate sales tax.) Billed orders will be charged postage and handling.

DISCOUNTS for quantity orders are available. Please write to the address below for information.

ALL ORDERS must include either the name of an individual or an official purchase order number. Please submit your order as follows:
Subscriptions: specify series and year subscription is to begin
Single copies: include individual title code (such as PF1)

MAIL ALL ORDERS TO:
Jossey-Bass Publishers
350 Sansome Street
San Francisco, California 94104-1310

FOR SINGLE-COPY SALES OUTSIDE OF THE UNITED STATES CONTACT:
Maxwell Macmillan International Publishing Group
866 Third Avenue
New York, New York 10022-6221

FOR SUBSCRIPTION SALES OUTSIDE OF THE UNITED STATES, contact any international subscription agency or Jossey-Bass directly.